4/04

EVERYMAN,
I WILL GO WITH THEE
AND BE THY GUIDE,
IN THY MOST NEED
TO GO BY THY SIDE

EVERYMAN'S LIBRARY
POCKET POETS

Doggerel

Poems About Dogs

Selected and edited by
Carmela Ciuraru

EVERYMAN'S LIBRARY

POCKET POETS

Alfred A. Knopf · New York · London · Toronto

THIS IS A BORZOI BOOK

PUBLISHED BY ALFRED A. KNOPF

This selection by Carmela Ciuraru first published in
Everyman's Library, 2003
Copyright © 2003 by Everyman's Library
A list of acknowledgments to copyright owners appears at the back
of this volume.

All rights reserved under International and Pan-American Copyright
Conventions. Published in the United States by Alfred A. Knopf, a
division of Random House, Inc., New York, and simultaneously in
Canada by Random House of Canada Limited, Toronto. Distributed by
Random House, Inc., New York. Published in the United Kingdom by
Everyman's Library, Gloucester Mansions, 140A Shaftesbury Avenue,
London WC2H 8HD.

www.randomhouse.com/everymans

ISBN 1-4000-4037-X (US)
1-84159-756-2 (UK)

A CIP catalogue record for this book is available from the British Library

Typography by Peter B. Willberg

Typeset in the UK by AccComputing, North Barrow, Somerset

Printed and bound in Germany
by GGP Media, Pössneck

CONTENTS

ON THE VIRTUES OF PARTICULAR BREEDS

8

10

11

FOREWORD

There are millions of dog owners the world over, and millions more who don't have a dog but yearn for one. If you've picked up this book, you're likely to be one or the other—even if you don't believe in the sentimental notion of the dog as man's best friend. Yet there's a case to be made for dogs being the ultimate companions. It's true that our friends stick with us despite our many flaws, and that dogs don't seem to know we *have* any flaws. But the fact is, we often behave badly with friends, including our best ones; we break promises and disappoint. We accept as a fact of life that people are often preoccupied or self-absorbed. As for dogs—unless immersed in tracking a scent, greeting another dog, or perhaps searching for scraps of food—generally they can be counted on to be at our side when we need them, and enthusiastically so. Isn't that kind of loyalty the mark of a true friend? Regarding the existence of traitorous dogs, the great humorist James Thurber wrote: "I have been double-crossed by dogs sixteen or eighteen times; eighteen, I believe. But I find in going back over these instances that in every case the fault really lay with me."

I have always loved dogs, and, aside from a miniature schnauzer named Schnitzel who bit me when I was eight years old, dogs have always loved me. They are often drawn to me as if to a fellow dog. A common encounter goes like this: a dog I have never met sees me from across the street, wags its tail excitedly, and yanks its bewildered owner over to greet me. Or I pass a dog on the sidewalk, smile at it, and look back to find that the dog has stopped in its tracks to stare at me, ears and tail at full alert.

Of course I am hardly alone in my dog love. Dogs have been adored for centuries, in life and in literature, and rightly so. This collection of poems spans more than five hundred years, offering up dogs at their best and (still lovable) worst. They are celebrated in puppyhood, admired for their abilities to hunt and protect, and fondly recalled in moving elegies. They are appreciated in all their variety, in verse tributes to the greyhound, Irish setter, St Bernard, Scottish terrier, and the pug. And they are honored for their ability, whether pure-breed or mongrel, to make us laugh when we really need to. With a chase of their own tail, dogs remind us not to take ourselves too seriously.

Some poems in the collection strike a more serious note, expressing gratitude for companionship in lonely moments, or paying tribute to beloved dogs that have died. Others, such as Don Marquis' "Confession of a Glutton," describe hilariously what dogs are capable of doing in our absence, like indiscriminately devouring everything in sight: "after i ate my dinner then i ate /

part of a shoe / i found some archies by a bathroom pipe / and ate them too / i ate some glue / i ate a bone that had got nice and ripe / six weeks buried in the ground / I ate a little mousie that i found . . ." And Karen Shepard's "Birch" celebrates a dog's generous offer to assist in finishing a meal: "You gonna eat that? / You gonna eat that? / You gonna eat that? / I'll eat that."

So sit. Stay. Lie down. Roll over. And appreciate what dogs can teach us about friendship, devotion, mischief, and, among other things, the art of untroubled sleep.

CARMELA CIURARU

MOST LOYAL AND
NOBLE COMPANION

AN INTRODUCTION TO DOGS

The dog is man's best friend.
He has a tail on one end.
Up in front he has teeth.
And four legs underneath.

Dogs like to bark.
They like it best after dark.
They not only frighten prowlers away
But also hold the sandman at bay.

A dog that is indoors
To be let out implores.
You let him out and what then?
He wants back in again.

Dogs display reluctance and wrath
If you try to give them a bath.
They bury bones in hideaways
And half the time they trot sideways.

Dogs in the country have fun.
They run and run and run.
But in the city this species
Is dragged around on leashes.

Dogs are upright as a steeple
And much more loyal than people.
Well people may be reprehensibler
But that's probably because they are sensibler.

THE POWER OF THE DOG

There is sorrow enough in the natural way
From men and women to fill our day;
And when we are certain of sorrow in store,
Why do we always arrange for more?
Brothers and Sisters, I bid you beware
Of giving your heart to a dog to tear.

Buy a pup and your money will buy
Love unflinching that cannot lie—
Perfect passion and worship fed
By a kick in the ribs or a pat on the head.
Nevertheless it is hardly fair
To risk your heart for a dog to tear.

When the fourteen years which Nature permits
Are closing in asthma, or tumour, or fits,
And the vet's unspoken prescription runs
To lethal chambers or loaded guns,
Then you will find—it's your own affair—
But . . . you've given your heart to a dog to tear.

When the body that lived at your single will,
With its whimper of welcome, is stilled (how still!);
When the spirit that answered your every mood
Is gone—wherever it goes—for good,

You will discover how much you care,
And will give your heart to a dog to tear.

We've sorrow enough in the natural way,
When it comes to burying Christian clay.
Our loves are not given, but only lent,
At compound interest of cent per cent.
Though it is not always the case, I believe,
That the longer we've kept 'em, the more do we grieve:
For, when debts are payable, right or wrong,
A short-time loan is as bad as a long—
So why in—Heaven (before we are there)
Should we give our hearts to a dog to tear?

THE DOG

I like a dog at my feet when I read,
Whatever his size or whatever his breed.
A dog now and then that will nuzzle my hand
As though I were the greatest of men in the land,
And trying to tell me it's pleasant to be
On such intimate terms with a fellow like me.

I like a dog at my side when I eat,
I like to give him a bit of my meat;
And though mother objects and insists it is bad
To let dogs in the dining room, still I am glad
To behold him stretched out on the floor by my chair.
It's cheering to see such a faithful friend there.

A dog leads a curious life at the best.
By the wag of his tail is his pleasure expressed.
He pays a high tribute to man when he stays
True to his friend to the end of his days.
And I wonder sometimes if it happens to be
That dogs pay no heed of the faults which men see.

Should I prove a failure; should I stoop to wrong;
Be weak at a time when I should have been strong,
Should I lose my money, the gossips would sneer
And fill with my blundering many an ear,
But still, as I opened my door, I should see
My dog wag his tail with a welcome for me.

EDGAR A. GUEST

UNDERSTANDING

Sometimes it seems as if a dog can sense
One's thoughts more quickly than a human can;
They know the moments that are dark and tense—
When worries have upset life's general plan.
And I have seen them gazing into space
At such a time, as if they almost knew
That any gesture would be out of place
Unless one asked for it. How very few
Of all the wise and learned of earth possess
This strange, uncanny power to understand
Man's deepest moods of utter loneliness,
When naught but silence meets the heart's demand.

THE BEST FRIEND

If I was sad, then he had grief, as well—
Seeking my hands with soft insistent paw,
Searching my face with anxious eyes that saw
More than my halting, human speech could tell;
Eyes wide with wisdom, fine, compassionate—
Dear, loyal one, that knew not wrong nor hate.

If I made merry—then how he would strive
To show his joy; "Good master, let's to play,
The world is ours," that gladsome bark would say;
"Just yours and mine—'tis fun to be alive!"
Our world . . . four walls above the city's din,
My crutch the bar that ever held us in.

Whate'er my mood—the fretful word, or sweet,
The swift command, the wheedling undertone,
His faith was fixed, his love was mine, alone,
His heaven was here at my slow crippled feet:
Oh, friend thrice-lost; oh, fond heart unassailed,
Ye taught me trust when man's dull logic failed.

ARGUS

When wise Ulysses, from his native coast
Long kept by wars, and long by tempests tost,
Arrived at last—poor, old, disguised, alone,
To all his friends and ev'n his queen unknown,
Changed as he was, with age, and toils, and cares,
Furrowed his rev'rend face, and white his hairs,
In his own palace forced to ask his bread,
Scorned by those slaves his former bounty fed,
Forgot of all his own domestic crew,
His faithful dog his rightful master knew!
Unfed, unhoused, neglected, on the clay,
Like an old servant, now cashiered, he lay;
And though ev'n then expiring on the plain,
Touched with resentment of ungrateful man,
And longing to behold his ancient lord again.
Him when he saw, he rose, and crawled to meet,
('Twas all he could), and fawned, and kissed his feet,
Seized with dumb joy; then falling by his side,
Owned his returning lord, looked up, and died.

TRAY, THE EXEMPLAR

My dog (the trustiest of his kind)
With gratitude inflames my mind;
I mark his true, his faithful way,
And in my service copy Tray.

VERSE FOR A CERTAIN DOG

Such glorious faith as fills your limpid eyes,
  Dear little friend of mine, I never knew.
All-innocent are you, and yet all-wise.
  (For Heaven's sake, stop worrying that shoe!)
You look about, and all you see is fair;
  This mighty globe was made for you alone.
Of all the thunderous ages, you're the heir.
  (Get off the pillow with that dirty bone!)

A skeptic world you face with steady gaze;
  High in young pride you hold your noble head;
Gayly you meet the rush of roaring days.
  (*Must* you eat puppy biscuit on the bed?)
Lancelike your courage, gleaming swift and strong,
  Yours the white rapture of a wingèd soul,
Yours is a spirit like a May-day song.
  (God help you, if you break the goldfish bowl!)

"Whatever is, is good"—your gracious creed.
  You wear your joy of living like a crown.
Love lights your simplest act, your every deed.
  (Drop it, I tell you—put that kitten down!)
You are God's kindliest gift of all—a friend.
  Your shining loyalty unflecked by doubt,
You ask but leave to follow to the end.
  (Couldn't you wait until I took you out?)

YOUR FACE ON THE DOG'S NECK

It is early afternoon.
You sit on the grass
with your rough face on the dog's neck.
Right now
you are both as still as a snapshot.
That infectious dog ought to let a fly bother her,
ought to run out in an immense field,
chasing rabbits and skunks,
mauling the cats, licking insects off her rump,
and stop using you up.
My darling, why do you lean on her so?
I would touch you,
that pulse brooding under your Madras shirt,
each shoulder the most well built house,
the arms, thin birches that do not escape the breeze,
the white teeth that have known me,
that wait at the bottom of the brook
and the tongue, my little fish! . . .
but you are stopped in time.

So I will speak of your eyes
although they are closed.
Tell me, where is each stubborn-colored iris?
Where are the quick pupils that make
the floor tilt under me?

I see only the lids, as tough as riding boots.
Why have your eyes gone into their own room?
Goodnight they are saying
from their little leathery doors.
Or shall I sing of eyes
that have been ruined with mercy and lust
and once with your own death
when you lay bubbling like a caught fish,
sucking on the manufactured oxygen?
Or shall I sing of eyes
that are resting so near the hair
of that hateful animal?
Love twists me, a Spanish flute plays in my blood,
and yet I can see only
your little sleep, an empty place.

But when your eyes open
against the wool stink of her thick hair,
against the faintly sickening neck of that dog,
whom I envy like a thief,
what will I ask?
Will I speak up saying,
there is a hurried song, a certain seizure
from which I gasp?
Or will your eyes lie in wait,
little field mice nestling on their paws?
Perhaps they will say nothing,

perhaps they will be dark and leaden,
having played their own game
somewhere else,
somewhere far off.

Oh, I have learned them and know that
when they open and glance at me
I will turn like a little dancer
and then, quite simply,
and all by myself,
I will fall,
bound to some mother/father,
bound to your sight,
bound for nowhere
and everywhere.
Or, perhaps, my darling,
because it is early afternoon,
I will forget that my voice is full of good people,
forget how my legs could sprawl on the terrace,
forget all that the birds might witness,
the torn dress, the shoes lost in the arbor,
while the neighbor's lawnmower bites and spits out
some new little rows of innocent grass.
Certainly,
I need not speak of it at all.
I will crouch down
and put my cheek near you,

accepting this spayed and flatulent bitch you hold,
letting my face rest in an assembled tenderness
on the old dog's neck.

DOG-GOD

To the railroad tracks at the bottom of summer
where weeds flourished, I return.

Flat-chested girl in a soiled T-shirt, I liked
the gully's privacy and the rank smell there

where I found dimes flattened by trains and milky
marbles, and once a rusty knife.

I must have reached for a trinket
in the grass when the collie's narrow muzzle

came close, the tricolored wedge of her head a foreign
    flag.
My first thought—*I have to return her*—I pushed aside

and stood still so she would stay and I could touch
the rich black hair that shone on her. She didn't run
    away.

To test her, I jogged up the hill and she followed,
    friendly,
like the TV dog, and when she sat, I sat, flushed with
    my amazing

luck, and wondering how long it might last, the whole
summer, maybe. I stroked her white breast and said
    Scotland out loud.

She cocked her head as if I'd conjured, with a charm,
    her name
or home, or a place we'd visit that afternoon. At a
    stream,

she drank, and the sound of her lapping excited a new
    desire
to master what is beautiful and guileless and mute.

MAN AND DOG

Who's this—alone with stone and sky?
It's only my old dog and I—
It's only him; it's only me;
Alone with stone and grass and tree.

What share we most—we two together?
Smells, and awareness of the weather.
What is it makes us more than dust?
My trust in him; in me his trust.

Here's anyhow one decent thing
That life to man and dog can bring;
One decent thing, remultiplied
Till earth's last dog and man have died.

GROWING DARK

The grass shakes.
Smoke streaks, no,
cloud strokes.
The dogs are fed.
Their licenses
clank on pottery.
The phone rings.
And is answered.
The pond path
is washed-out grass
between green
winter cover.
Last night in
bed I read.
You came to
my room and
said, "Isn't
the world
terrible?" "My
dear . . ." I
said. It could be
and has been
worse. So
beautiful and
things keep getting

in between. When
I was young I
hurt others. Now,
others have hurt
me. In the night
I thought I heard
a dog bark.
Racking sobs.
Poor guy. Yet,
I got my sleep.

CUSTODIAN

Every spring when the ice goes out
black commas come scribbling across the shallows.
Soon they sprout forelegs.
Slowly they absorb their tails
and by mid-June, full-voiced, announce themselves.

Enter our spotted dog.
Every summer, tense with the scent of them,
tail arced like a pointer's but wagging
in anticipation, he stalks his frogs
two hundred yards clockwise around
the perimeter of this mucky pond,
then counterclockwise, an old pensioner
happy in his work.

Once every ten or so pounces
he succeeds, carries his captive north
in his soft mouth, uncorks him on the grass,
and then sits, head cocked, watching the slightly
dazed amphibian hop back to sanctuary.

Over the years the pond's inhabitants
seem to have grown accustomed
to this ritual of capture and release.
They ride untroubled in the wet pocket

of the dog's mouth, disembark in the meadow
like hitchhikers, and strike out again for home.

I have seen others of his species kill
and swallow their catch and then be seized
with violent retchings. I have seen children
corner polliwogs in the sun-flecked hollow
by the green rock and lovingly squeeze
the life out of them in their small fists.
I have seen the great blue heron swoop in
time after wing-slapping time to carry
frogs back to the fledglings in the rookery.

Nothing is to be said here
of need or desire. No moral arises
nor is this, probably, purgatory.
We have this old dog,
custodian of an ancient race of frogs,
doing what he knows how to do
and we too, taking and letting go,
that same story.

MY COMFORTER

The world had all gone wrong that day
   And tired and in despair,
Discouraged with the ways of life,
   I sank into my chair.

A soft caress fell on my cheek,
   My hands were thrust apart.
And two big sympathizing eyes
   Gazed down into my heart.

I had a friend; what cared I now
   For fifty worlds? I knew
One heart was anxious when I grieved—
   My dog's heart, loyal, true.

"God bless him," breathed I soft and low,
   And hugged him close and tight.
One lingering lick upon my ear
   And we were happy—quite.

FIDELITY OF THE DOG

A barking sound the shepherd hears,
　　A cry as of a dog or fox;
He halts, and searches with his eyes
　　Among the scattered rocks:
And now at distance can discern
A stirring in a brake of fern;
And instantly a dog is seen,
Glancing through that covert green.

The dog is not of mountain breed;
　　Its motions too are wild and shy;
With something, as the shepherd thinks,
　　Unusual in its cry.
Nor is there anyone in sight
All round, in hollow, or on height;
Nor shout, nor whistle, strikes his ear;
What is the creature doing here?

It was a cove, a huge recess,
　　That keeps till June December's snow;
A lofty precipice in front,
　　A silent tarn below!
Far in the bosom of Helvellyn,
Remote from public road or dwelling,
Pathway, or cultivated land,
From trace of human foot or hand.

There sometimes doth a leaping fish
    Send through the tarn a lonely cheer;
The crags repeat the raven's croak,
    In symphony austere;
Thither the rainbow comes—the cloud—
And mists that spread the flying shroud;
And sunbeams, and the sounding blast,
That if it could would hurry past;
But that enormous barrier binds it fast.

Not free from boding thoughts, awhile
    The shepherd stood; then makes his way
Towards the dog, o'er rocks and stones,
    As quickly as he may;
Not far had gone before he found
A human skeleton on the ground;
The appall'd discoverer with a sigh,
Looks round to learn the history.

From those abrupt and perilous rocks
    The man had fall'n, that place of fear!
At length upon the shepherd's mind
    It breaks and all is clear;
He instantly recalled the name,
And who he was and whence he came;
Remember'd too the very day
On which the traveller pass'd this way.

But hear a wonder, for whose sake
    This lamentable tale I tell!
A lasting monument of words
    This wonder merits well.
The dog which still was hovering nigh,
Repeating the same timid cry,
This dog had been, through three months' space,
A dweller in that savage place.

Yes, proof was plain that since the day,
    When this ill-fated traveller died,
The dog had watched about the spot,
    Or by his master's side:
How nourish'd here through such long time,
He knows who gave that love sublime;
And gave that strength of feeling great
Above all human estimate.

TO FLUSH, MY DOG

Loving friend, the gift of one
Who her own true faith has run
    Through thy lower nature,
Be my benediction said
With my hand upon thy head,
    Gentle fellow creature!

Like a lady's ringlets brown,
Flow thy silken ears adown
    Either side demurely
Of thy silver-suited breast,
Shining out from all the rest
    Of thy body purely.

Darkly brown thy body is,
Till the sunshine striking this
    Alchemize its dullness,
When the sleek curls manifold
Flash all over into gold,
    With a burnished fullness.

Underneath my stroking hand,
Startled eyes of hazel bland
    Kindling, growing larger,
Up thou leapest with a spring

Full of prank and curveting,
    Leaping like a charger.

Leap! thy broad tail waves a light,
Leap! thy slender feet are bright,
    Canopied in fringes;
Leap—those tasselled ears of thine
Flicker strangely, fair and fine,
    Down their golden inches.

Yet, my pretty, sportive friend,
Little is't to such an end
    That I praise thy rareness!
Other dogs may be thy peers
Haply in these drooping ears,
    And this glossy fairness.

But of *thee* it shall be said,
This dog watched beside a bed
    Day and night unweary,—
Watched within a curtained room,
Where no sunbeam brake the gloom
    Round the sick and dreary.

Roses, gathered for a vase,
In that chamber died apace,
    Beam and breeze resigning;

This dog only, waited on,
Knowing that when light is gone
   Love remains for shining.

*   *   *

Other dogs of loyal cheer
Bounded at the whistle clear,
   Up the woodside hieing;
This dog only, watched in reach
Of a faintly uttered speech,
   Or a louder sighing.

And if one or two quick tears
Dropped upon his glossy ears,
   Or a sigh came double,—
Up he sprang in eager haste,
Fawning, fondling, breathing fast,
   In a tender trouble.

*   *   *

Therefore to this dog will I,
Tenderly not scornfully,
   Render praise and favour:
With my hand upon his head,
Is my benediction said
   Therefore, and for ever.

*   *   *

Blessings on thee, dog of mine,
Pretty collars make thee fine,
   Sugared milk make fat thee!
Pleasures wag on in thy tail,
Hands of gentle motion fail
   Nevermore, to pat thee!

Downy pillow take thy head,
Silken coverlid bestead,
   Sunshine help thy sleeping!
No fly's buzzing wake thee up,
No man break thy purple cup,
   Set for drinking deep in.

     *   *   *

Mock I thee, in wishing weal?—
Tears are in my eyes to feel
   Thou art made so straitly,
Blessing needs must straiten too,—
Little canst thou joy or do,
   Thou who lovest *greatly*.

Yet be blessèd to the height
Of all good and all delight
   Pervious to thy nature;
Only *loved* beyond that line,
With a love that answers thine,
   Loving fellow creature!

ELIZABETH BARRETT BROWNING   47

PUPPY LOVE

HIS APOLOGIES

Master, this is Thy Servant. He is rising eight weeks old.
He is mainly Head and Tummy. His legs are
　　uncontrolled.
But Thou hast forgiven his ugliness, and settled him
　　on Thy knee...
Art Thou content with Thy servant? He is *very* comfy
　　with Thee.

Master, behold a Sinner! He hath committed a wrong.
He hath defiled Thy Premises through being kept in
　　too long.
Wherefore his nose has been rubbed in the dirt, and his
　　self-respect has been bruisèd.
Master, pardon Thy Sinner, and see he is properly
　　loosèd.

Master—again Thy Sinner! This that was once
　　Thy Shoe,
He has found and taken and carried aside, as fitting
　　matter to chew.
Now there is neither blacking nor tongue, and the
　　House-maid has us in tow.
Master, remember Thy Servant is young, and tell her
　　to let him go!

Master, extol Thy Servant, he has met a most
    Worthy Foe!
There has been fighting all over the Shop—and into
    the Shop also!
Till cruel umbrellas parted the strife (or I might have
    been choking him yet).
But Thy Servant has had the Time of his Life—and
    now shall we call on the vet?

Master, behold Thy Servant! Strange children came
    to play,
And because they fought to caress him Thy Servant
    wentedst away.
But now that the Little Beasts have gone, he has
    returned to see
(Brushed—with his Sunday collar on) what they left
    over from tea.

Master, pity Thy Servant! He is deaf and three parts
    blind.
He cannot catch The Commandments. He cannot read
    Thy Mind.
Oh, leave him not to his loneliness nor make him that
    kitten's scorn.
He hath none other God than Thee since the year that
    he was born.

Lord, look down on Thy Servant! Bad things have
    come to pass.
There is no heat in the midday sun, nor health in the
    wayside grass.
His bones are full of an old disease—his torments run
    and increase.
Lord, make haste with Thy Lightnings and grant him
    a quick release!

RUDYARD KIPLING   53

HOW IT BEGAN

They struggled their legs and blindly loved, those puppies
inside my jacket as I walked through town. They crawled
for warmth and licked each other—their poor mother
dead, and one kind boy to save them. I spread
my arms over their world and hurried along.

At Ellen's place I knocked and waited—the tumult
invading my sleeves, all my jacket alive.
When she came to the door we tumbled—black, white
gray, hungry—all over the living room floor
together, rolling, whining, happy, and blind.

From THE CHASE

                    Soon as the tender dam
Has formed them with her tongue, with pleasure view
The marks of their renowned progenitors,
Sure pledge of triumphs yet to come. All these
Select with joy; but to the merciless flood
Expose the dwindling refuse, nor o'erload
Th' indulgent mother. If thy heart relent,
Unwilling to destroy, a nurse provide,
And to the foster parent give the care
Of thy superfluous brood; she'll cherish kind
The alien offspring; pleased thou shalt behold
Her tenderness and hospitable love.
If frolic now and playful they desert
Their gloomy cell, and on the verdant turf,
With nerves improved, pursue the mimic chase,
Coursing around; unto the choicest friends
Commit thy valued prize: the rustic dames
Shall at thy kennel wait, and in their laps
Receive thy growing hopes, with many a kiss
Caress, and dignify their little charge
With some great title, and resounding name
Of high import.

But cautious here observe
To check their youthful ardour, nor permit
The inexperienced younker, immature,
Alone to range the woods, or haunt the brakes
Where dodging conies sport—his nerves unstrung,
And strength unequal; the laborious chase
Shall stint his growth, and his rash, forward youth
Contract such vicious habits as thy care
And late correction never shall reclaim.

When to full strength arrived, mature and bold,
Conduct them to the field; not all at once,
But as thy cooler prudence shall direct,
Select a few, and form them by degrees
To stricter discipline. With these consort
The staunch and steady sages of thy pack,
By long experience versed in all the wiles
And subtle doublings of the various chase.
Easy the lesson of the youthful train
When instinct prompts, and when example guides.
If the too forward younker at the head
Press boldly on in wanton sportive mood,
Correct his haste, and let him feel abashed
The ruling whip. But if he stoop behind
In wary modest guise, to his own nose

Confiding sure, give him full scope to work
His winding way, and with thy voice applaud
His patience and his care; soon shalt thou view
The hopeful pupil leader of his tribe,
And all the listening pack attend his call.

DRINK, PUPPY, DRINK
Hunting Song

Here's to the fox in his earth below the rocks!
    And here's to the line that we follow,
And here's to the hound with his nose upon the ground,
    Tho' merrily we whoop and we holloa!

    Chorus
    Then drink, puppy, drink, and let every puppy drink,
        That is old enough to lap and to swallow,
    For he'll grow into a hound, so we'll pass the bottle
    round,
        And merrily we'll whoop and we'll holloa.

Here's to the horse, and the rider, too, of course;
    And here's to the rally o' the hunt, boys;
Here's a health to every friend, who can struggle to
    the end,
    And here's to the Tally-ho in front, boys.
    Chorus

Here's to the gap, and the timber that we rap,
    Here's to the white thorn, and the black, too;
And here's to the pace that puts life into the chase
    And the fence that gives a moment to the pack, too.
    Chorus

Oh! the pack is staunch and true, now they run from
    scent to view,
  And it's worth the risk to life and limb and neck,
    boys;
To see them drive and stoop till they finish with
    "Who-whoop".
  Forty minutes on the grass without a check, boys.
    Chorus

THE HOUND OF ULSTER

Little boy
Will you stop
And take a look
In the puppy shop—
Dogs blue and liver
Noses aquiver
Little dogs big dogs
Dogs for sport and pleasure
Fat dogs meagre dogs
Dogs for lap and leisure.
Do you see that wire-haired terrier?
Could anything be merrier?
Do you see that Labrador retriever?
His name is Belvoir.
     Thank you courteous stranger, said the child,
     By your words I am beguiled,
     But tell me I pray
     What lurks in the grey
     Cold shadows at the back of the shop?
Little boy do not stop
Come away
From the puppy shop.
For the Hound of Ulster lies tethered there
Cuchulain tethered by his golden hair
His eyes are closed and his lips are pale
Hurry little boy he is not for sale.

DOG DAYS

Franz Schubert, in this life, is six weeks old in the body
of a chocolate-brown labrador who reminds me that risk
is extra life when he takes my hand easily in his
mouth and leads me through new teeth and a snowfall
     blanking town.
I think this snow must be able to lift two children, who
are fighting, out of their argumentative skins and make

a day so bright, it winces. What is ever this willing?
This vibrant dog with me, loving my hand as if it could
delay his life a little, makes me want to be him and
his newborn smile: play-ferocious on the way to
     heartbreak.
Reaching it back to the perfect wet arc of young bone that
forces itself into the roof of Franz's mouth, my hand

follows with my body and enters him. It is summer
again in the canoes. The man I come to when he calls,
approaches, first on a wrinkle of water, then as
himself, and we are ready to go. Franz, good dog, inside
me this is life I did not choose and you have yours, ready.

ON THE VIRTUES OF
PARTICULAR BREEDS

DOGS AND WEATHER

I'd like a different dog
    For every kind of weather—
A narrow greyhound for a fog,
    A wolfhound strange and white,
With a tail like a silver feather
    To run with in the night,
When snow is still, and winter stars are bright.

In the fall I'd like to see
    In answer to my whistle,
A golden spaniel look at me.
    But best of all for rain
A terrier, hairy as a thistle,
    To trot with fine disdain
Beside me down the soaked, sweet-smelling lane.

THE DOG PARADE

In times of calm or hurricane, in days of sun or shower,
The dog-paraders, each and all, observe the canine hour,

And, some with pups in single leash, and some with
    tugging pairs,
Take out their poodles, pointers, Poms and frisky
    wirehairs.

The Scotties patter doggedly, sedate and wistful-eyed,
The setters leap, the spaniels romp, the Great Danes
    walk in pride.

And here are shaggy shepherd dogs, those heroes of the
    farm,
And there a Russian wolfhound comes with quaint,
    Slavonic charm.

Or one may note a brindled bull, less frivolous than most,
Who, like a faithful sentinel, is ever at his post.

But still the dog-paraders march, exchanging friendly
    bows,
Escorting dachshunds, Dobermans, Dalmatians, Pekes
    and chows.

And still in placid dignity that nothing can disturb,
They lead their charges down the street, and sometimes
    to the curb.

66   ARTHUR GUITERMAN

ADVICE TO A DOG PAINTER

Happiest of the spaniel race,
Painter, with thy colours grace,
Draw his forehead large and high,
Draw his blue and humid eye;
Draw his neck, so smooth and round,
Little neck with ribands bound;
And the musely swelling breast
Where the Loves and Graces rest;
And the spreading, even back,
Soft, and sleek, and glossy black;
And the tail that gently twines,
Like the tendrils of the vines;
And the silky twisted hair,
Shadowing thick the velvet ear;
Velvet ears which, hanging low,
O'er the veiny temples flow.

THE IRISH GREYHOUND

Behold this Creature's form and state,
Which Nature therefore did create,
That to the World might be expressed
What mien there can be in a Beast;
And that we in this shape may find
A Lion of another kind,
For this Heroic beast does seem
In Majesty to Rival him,
And yet vouchsafes to Man to show
Both service and submission too.
From whence we this distinction have,
That Beast is fierce, but that is brave.
This Dog hath so himself subdued
That hunger cannot make him rude:
And his behaviour does confess
True Courage dwells with Gentleness.
With sternest Wolves he dares engage,
And acts on them successful rage.
Yet too much courtesy may chance
To put him out of countenance.
When in his opposer's blood,
Fortune hath made his virtue good;
This Creature from an act so brave
Grows not more sullen, but more grave.
Man's Guard he would be, not his sport,

Believing he hath ventured for 't;
But yet no blood or shed or spent
Can ever make him insolent.
Few men of him to do great things have learned,
And, when th' are done, to be so unconcerned.

HAMISH: A SCOTS TERRIER

Little lad, little lad, and who's for an airing,
Who's for the river and who's for a run;
Four little pads to go fitfully faring,
Looking for trouble and calling it fun?
Down in the sedges the water-rats revel,
Up in the woods there are bunnies at play,
With a weather-eye wide for a Little Black Devil,
But the Little Black Devil won't come to-day.
To-day at the farm the ducks may slumber,
To-day may the tabbies an anthem raise,
Rat and rabbit beyond all number
To-day untroubled may go their ways:
To-day is an end of the shepherd's labour,
No more will the sheep be hunted astray,
And the Irish terrier, foe and neighbour,
Says, "What's old Hamish about to-day?"

Ay, what indeed, in the nether spaces
Will the soul of a little black dog despair?
Will the Quiet Folk scare him with shadow faces,
And how will he tackle the strange beasts there?
Tail held high, I'll warrant, and bristling,
Marching stoutly, if sore afraid,
Padding it steadily, softly whistling—
That's how the Little Black Devil was made.

Then well-a-day for a "cantie callant,"
A heart of gold and a soul of glee—
Sportsman, gentleman, squire and gallant—
Teacher maybe of you and me.
Spread the turf on him high and level,
Grave him a headstone clear and true,
"Here lies Hamish, the Little Black Devil,
And half of the heart of his Mistress too."

MY BRINDLE BULL-TERRIER

My brindle bull-terrier, loving and wise,
With his little screw-tail and his wonderful eyes,
With his white little breast and his white little paws
Which, alas! he mistakes very often for claws;
With his sad little gait as he comes from the fight
When he feels that he hasn't done all that he might;
Oh, so fearless of man, yet afraid of a frog,
My near little, queer little, dear little dog!

He shivers and shivers and shakes with the cold;
He huddles and cuddles, though three summers old,
And forsaking the sunshine, endeavors to rove
With his cold little worriments under the stove!

At table, his majesty, dying for meat,—
Yet never despising a lump that is sweet,—
Sits close by my side with his head on my knee
And steals every good resolution from me!

How can I withhold from those worshipping eyes
A small bit of something that stealthily flies
Down under the table and into his mouth
As I tell my dear neighbor of life in the South.

My near little, queer little, dear little dog,
So fearless of man, yet afraid of a frog!
The nearest and queerest and dearest of all
The race that is loving and winning and small;
The sweetest, most faithful, the truest and best
Dispenser of merriment, love and unrest!

THE DOG AND THE WATER-LILY

The noon was shady, and soft airs
    Swept Ouse's silent tide,
When, 'scaped from literary cares,
    I wander'd on his side.

My spaniel, prettiest of his race,
    And high in pedigree,—
(Two nymphs adorn'd with every grace
    That spaniel found for me,)

Now wanton'd lost in flags and reeds,
    Now, starting into sight,
Pursued the swallow o'er the meads
    With scarce a slower flight.

It was the time when Ouse display'd
    His lilies newly blown;
Their beauties I intent survey'd,
    And one I wish'd my own.

With cane extended far I sought
    To steer it close to land;
But still the prize, though nearly caught,
    Escaped my eager hand.

Beau mark'd my unsuccessful pains
    With fix'd considerate face,

And puzzling set his puppy brains
    To comprehend the case.

But with a cherup clear and strong
    Dispersing all his dream,
I thence withdrew, and follow'd long
    The windings of the stream.

My ramble ended, I return'd;
    Beau, trotting far before,
The floating wreath again discern'd,
    And plunging left the shore.

I saw him with that lily cropp'd
    Impatient swim to meet
My quick approach, and soon he dropp'd
    The treasure at my feet.

Charm'd with the sight, "The world," I cried,
    "Shall hear of this thy deed;
My dog shall mortify the pride
    Of man's superior breed;

"But chief myself I will enjoin,
    Awake at duty's call,
To show a love as prompt as thine
    To Him who gives me all."

WILLIAM COWPER   75

TO A BLACK GREYHOUND

Shining black in the shining light,
    Inky black in the golden sun,
Graceful as the swallow's flight,
    Light as swallow, wingèd one,
Swift as driven hurricane—
    Double-sinewed stretch and spring,
Muffled thud of flying feet,
    See the black dog galloping,
    Hear his wild foot-beat.

See him lie when the day is dead,
    Black curves curled on the boarded floor.
Sleepy eyes, my sleepy-head—
    Eyes that were aflame before.
Gentle now, they burn no more;
    Gentle now and softly warm,
With the fire that made them bright
    Hidden—as when after storm
    Softly falls the night.

God of speed, who makes the fire—
    God of Peace, who lulls the same—
God who gives the fierce desire,
    Lust for blood as fierce as flame—
God who stands in Pity's name—

Many may ye be or less,
Ye who rule the earth and sun:
    Gods of strength and gentleness,
    Ye are ever one.

SHEEPDOG TRIALS IN HYDE PARK
For Robert Frost

A shepherd stands at one end of the arena.
Five sheep are unpenned at the other. His dog runs out
In a curve to behind them, fetches them straight to the
    shepherd,
Then drives the flock round a triangular course
Through a couple of gates and back to his master; two
Must be sorted there from the flock, then all five penned.
Gathering, driving away, shedding and penning
Are the plain words for the miraculous game.

An abstract game. What can the sheepdog make of such
Simplified terrain?—no hills, dales, bogs, walls, tracks,
Only a quarter-mile plain of grass, dumb crowds
Like crowds on hoardings around it, and behind them
Traffic or mounds of lovers and children playing.
Well, the dog is no landscape-fancier; his whole concern
Is with his master's whistle, and of course
With the flock—sheep are sheep anywhere for him.

The sheep are the chanciest element. Why, for instance,
Go through this gate when there's on either side of it
No wall or hedge but huge and viable space?
Why not eat the grass instead of being pushed around it?
Like blobs of quicksilver on a tilting board

The flock erratically runs, dithers, breaks up,
Is reassembled: their ruling idea is the dog;
And behind the dog, though they know it not yet, is a
    shepherd.

The shepherd knows that time is of the essence
But haste calamitous. Between dog and sheep
There is always an ideal distance, a perfect angle;
But these are constantly varying, so the man
Should anticipate each move through the dog, his
    medium.
The shepherd is the brain behind the dog's brain,
But his control of dog, like dog's of sheep,
Is never absolute—that's the beauty of it.

For beautiful it is. The guided missiles,
The black-and-white angels follow each quirk and jink of
The evasive sheep, play grandmother's steps behind
    them,
Freeze to the ground, or leap to head off a straggler
Almost before it knows that it wants to stray,
As if radar-controlled. But they are not machines—
You can feel them feeling mastery, doubt, chagrin:
Machines don't frolic when their job is done.

What's needfully done in the solitude of sheep-runs—
Those tough, real tasks—becomes this stylized game,
A demonstration of intuitive wit
Kept natural by the saving grace of error.
To lift, to fetch, to drive, to shed, to pen
Are acts I recognize, with all they mean
Of shepherding the unruly, for a kind of
Controlled woolgathering is my work too.

THE DACHSHUND

A Dachshund sniffing round a tree
    Made such a wondrous bend, sir,
He filled himself with mystery—
    Not knowing his own end, sir.

Some other dogs have keener sight,
    And some have greater strength, sir,
But no dogs manage, for their height,
    To have so much of length, sir.

One time—at least, so people say—
    One lost his tail by train, sir;
Yet two weeks passed until the day
    The sad news reached his brain, sir.

The Dachshund looks a little bit
    Like legs beneath a log, sir,
But once your eyes get used to it,
    You see that it's a dog, sir.

JOHN E. DONOVAN

THE DOG OF ST BERNARD'S

They tell that on St Bernard's mount,
  Where holy monks abide,
Still mindful of misfortune's claim,
  Though dead to all beside;

The weary, way-worn traveller
  Oft sinks beneath the snow;
For, were his faltering steps to bend,
  No track is left to show.

'Twas here, bewildered and alone,
  A stranger roamed at night;
His heart was heavy as his tread,
  His scrip alone was light.

Onward he pressed, yet many an hour
  He had not tasted food;
For many an hour he had not known
  Which way his footsteps trod;

And if the Convent's bell had rung
  To hail the pilgrims near,
It still had rung in vain for him—
  He was too far to hear.

And should the morning light disclose
    Its towers amid the snow,
To him 'twould be a mournful sight—
    He had not strength to go.

Valour could arm no mortal man
    That night to meet the storm;
No glow of pity could have kept
    A human bosom warm.

But obedience to a master's will
    Had taught the dog to roam,
And through the terrors of the waste
    To fetch the wanderer home.

He never loiters by the way,
    Nor lays him down to rest,
Nor seeks a refuge from the storm
    That pelts his generous breast.

And surely 'tis not less than joy
    That makes it throb so fast,
When he sees, extended on the snow,
    The wanderer found at last.

Eager emotion swelled his breast
    To tell the generous tale,
And he raised his voice to the loudest tone
    To bid the wanderer hail!

The pilgrim heard, he raised his head,
    And beheld the shaggy form,
With sudden fear he seized the gun
    That rested on his arm.

Fear gave him back his wasted strength,
    He took his aim too well,
The bullet bore the message home—
    The injured mastiff fell!

His eye was dimmed, his voice was still,
    And he tossed his head no more;
But his heart, though it ceased to throb with joy,
    Was generous as before.

For round his willing neck he bore
    A store of needful food,
That might support the traveller's strength
    On the yet remaining road.

So he heeded not his aching wound,
    But crawled to the traveller's side,
Marked with a look the way he came,
    Then shuddered, groaned, and died.

TO A POMERANIAN PUPPY
VALUED AT 2500 DOLLARS

Often as I strain and stew,
    Digging in these dirty ditches,
I have dared to think of you,
    You and all your riches.

Lackeys help you on and off;
    Silk's the stuff on which you're lying.
You have doctors when you cough,
    Priests when you are dying.

Wrapt in soft and costly furs,
    All sewed up with careful stitches,
You consort with proper curs
    And with perfumed bitches.

At your lightest, wheezy bark,
    Haughty women run to feed you;
Deaf to all things else, they hark,
    And, what's more, they heed you.

Guarded from the world, you grow
    Sleek and snug in pillowed niches;
You will never have to know
    Common ills or itches.

Lord, but things are queer and odd,
    Queerer still, with you to show it;
You're a lucky dog, by God,
    And you do not know it.

You don't sweat to struggle free,
    Work in rags and rotting breeches.
Puppy, have a laugh at me,
    Digging in the ditches.

MY FATHER'S IRISH SETTERS

Always throughout his life
(The parts of it I knew)
Two or three would be racing
Up stairs and down hallways,
Whining to take us walking,
Or caked with dirt, resigning
Keen ears to bouts of talk—
Until his third, last wife
Put down her little foot.
That splendid, thoroughbred
Lineage was penned
Safely out of earshot:
Fed, of course, and watered,
But never let out to run.
"Dear God," the new wife simpered,
Tossing her little head,
"Suppose they got run over—
Wouldn't *that* be the end?"

Each time I visited
(Once or twice a year)
I'd slip out, giving my word
Not to get carried away.
At the dogs' first sight of me
Far off—of anyone—

Began a joyous barking,
A russet-and-rapid-as-flame
Leaping, then whimpering lickings
Of face and hands through wire.
Like fire, like fountains leaping
With love and loyalty,
Put, were they, in safekeeping
By love, or for love's sake?
Dear heart, to love's own shame.
But loyalty transferred
Leaves famously slim pickings,
And no one's left to blame.

Divorced again, my father
(Hair white, face deeply scored)
Looked round and heaved a sigh.
The setters were nowhere.
Fleet muzzle, soulful eye
Dead lo! these forty winters?
Not so. Tonight in perfect
Lamplit stillness begin
With updraft from the worksheet,
Leaping and tongues, far-shining
Hearths of our hinterland:
Dour chieftain, maiden pining
Away for that lost music,
Her harpist's wild red hair...

Dear clan of Ginger and Finn,
As I go through your motions
(As they go through me, rather)
Love follows, pen in hand.

THE PROPERTIES OF A GOOD GREYHOUND

A greyhound should be headed like a Snake,
And necked like a Drake,
Footed like a Cat,
Tailed like a Rat,
Sidèd like a Team,
Chined like a Beam.

The first year he must learn to feed,
The second year to field him lead,
The third year he is fellow-like,
The fourth year there is none sike,
The fifth year he is good enough,
The sixth year he shall hold the plough,
The seventh year he will avail
Great bitches for to assail,
The eighth year lick ladle,
The ninth year cart saddle,
And when he is comen to that year
Have him to the tanner,
For the best hound that ever bitch had
At nine year he is full bad.

BARRY, THE ST BERNARD

                    When the storm
Rose, and the snow rolled on in ocean-waves,
When on his face the experienced traveller fell,
Sheltering his lips and nostrils with his hands,
Then all was changed; and, sallying with their pack
Into that blank of nature, they became
Unearthly beings. "Anselm, higher up,
Just where it drifts, a dog howls loud and long,
And now, as guided by a voice from Heaven,
Digs with his feet. That noble vehemence,
Whose can it be, but his who never erred?
A man lies underneath! Let us to work."

THE HAIRY DOG

My dog's so furry I've not seen
His face for years and years;
His eyes are buried out of sight,
I only guess his ears.

When people ask me for his breed,
I do not know or care;
He has the beauty of them all
Hidden beneath his hair.

O PUG!

To the Brownes' pug dog, on my lap, in their car,
coming home from Norfolk

O Pug, some people do not like you,
But I like you,
Some people say you do not breathe, you snore,
I don't mind,
One person says he is always conscious of your behind,
Is that your fault?

Your own people love you,
All the people in the family that owns you
Love you: Good pug, they cry, Happy pug,
Pug-come-for-a-walk.

You are an old dog now
And in all your life
You have never had cause for a moment's anxiety,
Yet,
In those great eyes of yours,
Those liquid and protuberant orbs,
Lies the shadow of immense insecurity. There
Panic walks.

Yes, yes, I know,
When your mistress is with you,
When your master
Takes you upon his lap,
Just then, for a moment,
Almost you are not frightened.

But at heart you are frightened, you always have been.

O Pug, obstinate old nervous breakdown,
In the midst of *so* much love,
And such comfort,
Still to feel unsafe and be afraid,

How one's heart goes out to you!

COMPENDIUM DACHSHUNDIUM

At first the bewhiskered professors did little more than
    smile
at the grad student's idea that dogs could determine an
    author's style,

but then it was confirmed that Dickinson had a dog
    Carlo
& that he was the interrupting sort & there was no way
    to show

that those dashes weren't just barks recorded on
    paper—
& soon the student was on Oprah & it was impossible
    to escape her

blithe declarations: Mystery of Henry James' Long
    Sentences
Solved! Daguerreotype of Dachshund Proves Its
    Existence!

At one conference she conceded that Proust might not
    have had
a pet, as no self-respecting animal would have let him
    linger that

long with a madeleine half-eaten in his fingers. Still,
    the effect
on contemporary writers was disastrous—one whose
    intellect

desperately needed the petting his Chihuahua was
    getting, threw
himself under a bus, & then there was the mystery
    writer who

refused to be categorized according to his pet & bought
    it
a puffy silver suit which showed only the animal's eyes
    & the tip

of its snout. Of course it soon came out that the dog
    was a poodle
(critics quickly learned to proffer a bone) & his sales
    dwindled—

after interviews with Carmela of Carmela's Canine
    Coifs, his penchant
for trimming clues into topiary had suddenly ceased to
    enchant.

PANEGYRIC FOR GEE

The anachronistic face of the bulldog,
the anachronistic, Churchillian face of the bulldog,
the anachronistic, Churchillian, gargoylean
face of the bulldog, the anachronistic, Churchillian,
gargoylean, Quasimodian face of the bulldog,
whose ears are silk purses,
whose eyes, like a bullfrog's, enlarge,
whose flat black wet gorilla's nose sucks the air
out of the dust, whose mouth is as wide
as a channel cat's feeding for years in solitude
on the bottom, whose two lower utter canines
show one at a time, bite that is worse than its bark,
whose slobber is the drool of herbivores,
whose brooding pose is the seal's,
who climbs and descends, who stands, who climbs
        again,
who at the top of the stairs in the morning dark
is beef-faced drowsy as the mastiff god—
the andiron-large front legs welded like doorstops to
        the paws—
who peers down from prehistory over the edge.
O gnomic skin and bone too big for a soul
squeezed from a root-slip in the earth,
O antediluvian noises in the throat,
O silences of staring straight ahead,

O dogtrot, O dreams of the chase ten yards and then a
 rest—.
To sleep by a bulldog is to return to the primal nasal
sleep of the drunk, the drunk whose carnal snore self-
 purifies
the breath with the sanctity of opera,
the rich deep long great breath of the animal breached
 but flying.
When my father slept he slept the sleep of a drunk
who'd have loved this bulldog, so stubborn at the
 forehead,
so set on plowing through to the conclusion of a door
too thick to pass, except in spirit,
whose singing sober voice alone breaks hearts.

IN PRAISE OF THE BASSET HOUND

This unlovely dog, with warts, and a terrible stink
common to the breed, legless as a walrus, teaches me
to pursue my life with devotion. Steadfast enthusiast
of fisher cat and vole, she relies now almost entirely
     on scent
and sings her hound's song of pleasure when we come
close enough for her to hear her name.
In snow above her shoulder, she tracks our skis,
when all we can see is her metronome tail
tipped in black, sweeping the horizon a mile back.
We keep her, incontinent, in an old shed behind the
     farmhouse,
a wire fence around her run. Warm days, nose in
     the air,
she sits like an old retiree in the sun, listening
to warblers build their spring nests.
Her warts ooze, her eyes rain green phlegm. Still,
I kiss her and hold her against my breast,
she who whelped twelve litters before someone
took pity and bought her from the breeder.
Never permitted to lick hand or face, she will not
disgrace her training and extend her tongue in play,
though I offer my cheek. Daily, she shows me
the meaning of character, loping painfully
on swollen paws. I apply salve to her scaley folds,

croon over her. Who among us has not been
moved by the magnificence of mute
creatures in their abundant, dying skin?

BEAGLES

That Boxing Day morning, I would hear the familiar,
    far-off gowls and gulders
over Keenaghan and Aughanlig
of a pack of beagles, old dogs disinclined to chase a car
    suddenly quite unlike

themselves, pups coming helter-skelter
across the ploughlands with all the chutzpah of veterans
of the trenches, their slate-greys, cinnamons, liver-
    browns, lemons, rusts, and violets

turning and twisting, unseen, across the fields,
their gowls and gulders turning and twisting after the
    twists and turns
of the great hare who had just now sauntered into the
    yard where I stood on tiptoe

astride my new Raleigh cycle,
his demeanour somewhat louche, somewhat
    lackadaisical
under the circumstances, what with him standing on
    tiptoe
as if to mimic me, standing almost as tall as I, looking
    as if he might for a moment put
himself in my place, thinking better of it, sloping off
    behind the lorry bed.

HAVE LEASH,
WILL WALK

AFTER AN ILLNESS, WALKING THE DOG

Wet things smell stronger,
and I suppose his main regret is that
he can sniff just one at a time.
In a frenzy of delight
he runs way up the sandy road—
scored by freshets after five days
of rain. Every pebble gleams, every leaf.

When I whistle he halts abruptly
and steps in a circle,
swings his extravagant tail.
Then he rolls and rubs his muzzle
in a particular place, while the drizzle
falls without cease, and Queen Anne's lace
and goldenrod bend low.

The top of the logging road stands open
and bright. Another day, before
hunting starts, we'll see how far it goes,
leaving word first at home.
The footing is ambiguous.

Soaked and muddy, the dog drops,
panting, and looks up with what amounts
to a grin. It's so good to be uphill with him,
nicely winded, and looking down on the pond.

A sound commences in my left ear
like the sound of the sea in a shell;
a downward vertiginous drag comes with it.

Time to head home. I wait
until we're nearly out to the main road
to put him back on the leash, and he
—the designated optimist—
imagines to the end that he is free.

THE WOODMAN'S DOG
From The Task

Forth goes the woodman, leaving unconcern'd
The cheerful haunts of man; to wield the axe
And drive the wedge, in yonder forest drear,
From morn to eve his solitary task.
Shaggy, and lean, and shrewd, with pointed ears
And tail cropp'd short, half lurcher and half cur—
His dog attends him. Close behind his heel
Now creeps he slow; and now, with many a frisk
Wide-scamp'ring, snatches up the drifted snow
With iv'ry teeth, or ploughs it with his snout;
Then shakes his powder'd coat, and barks for joy.

DOGS IN THE PARK

The precise yet furtive etiquette of dogs
Makes them ignore the whistle while they talk
In circles round each other, one-man bonds
Deferred in pauses of this man-made walk
To open vistas to a past of packs

That raven round the stuccoed terraces
And scavenge at the mouth of Stone Age caves;
What man proposes dog on his day disposes
In litter round both human and canine graves,
Then lifts his leg to wash the gravestones clean,

While simultaneously his eyes express
Apology and contempt; his master calls
And at the last and sidelong he returns,
Part heretic, part hack, and jumps and crawls
And fumbles to communicate and fails.

And then they leave the park, the leads are snapped
On to the spiky collars, the tails wag
For no known reason and the ears are pricked
To search through legendary copse and crag
For legendary creatures doomed to die
Even as they, the dogs, were doomed to live.

MY DOG IS NAMED FOR
ELIZABETH BISHOP

October. The first pricks of cold air in
the city morning. We walk, Liz and I,
up then down in the same uneven line.

Her ears as sharp as sharpened pencils,
she pulls me along her wayward travels.
She darts out headlong, paces ahead,

coming and going and leaving again,
the way shadows seem to meet the tops of heads,
dissolve and are newly elongated.

We like the early, early morning best.
Our view is, thankfully, how we left it.
Nothing has stirred yet, the news lies unread.

Except for the weather, it's all so still,
and no one is walking out of our world.

SATURDAY, 8:58 A.M.

The quilt of leaves, wet from a warm November
    shower
smells of the dirt it will mulch into.
The branches look empty. The empty sky
is full of stratus clouds pressing the air
like a great palm. This I imagine from walks with
and without you those years we thought,
counted on, the dog saving our marriage.
From a Manhattan studio I imagine you
in Prospect Park a few minutes after nine
when the park rangers ticket owners
whose dogs are still off-leash.
The air is bright even under the clouds.
I once thought I would stay with you
if only not to see you in such pain.

WALKING THE DOG

Two universes mosey down the street
Connected by love and a leash and nothing else.
Mostly I look at lamplight through the leaves
While he mooches along with tail up and snout down,
Getting a secret knowledge through the nose
Almost entirely hidden from my sight.

We stand while he's enraptured by a bush
Till I can't stand our standing any more
And haul him off; for our relationship
Is patience balancing to this side tug
And that side drag; a pair of symbionts
Contented not to think each other's thoughts.

What else we have in common's what he taught,
Our interest in shit. We know its every state
From steaming fresh through stink to nature's way
Of sluicing it downstreet dissolved in rain
Or drying it to dust that blows away.
We move along the street inspecting it.

His sense of it is keener far than mine,
And only when he finds the place precise
He signifies by sniffing urgently
And circles thrice about, and squats, and shits,
Whereon we both with dignity walk home
And just to show who's master I write the poem.

HOWARD NEMEROV   111

TO SLEEP AND
TO DREAM

A DOG SLEEPING ON MY FEET

Being his resting place,
I do not even tense
The muscles of a leg
Or I would seem to be changing.
Instead, I turn the page
Of the notebook, carefully not

Remembering what I have written,
For now, with my feet beneath him
Dying like embers,
The poem is beginning to move
Up through my pine-prickling legs
Out of the night wood,

Taking hold of the pen by my fingers.
Before me the fox floats lightly,
On fire with his holy scent.
All, all are running.
Marvelous is the pursuit,
Like a dazzle of nails through the ankles,

Like a twisting shout through the trees
Sent after the flying fox
Through the holes of logs, over streams
Stock-still with the pressure of moonlight.

My killed legs,
My legs of a dead thing, follow,

Quick as pins, through the forest,
And all rushes on into dark
And ends on the brightness of paper.
When my hand, which speaks in a daze
The hypnotized language of beasts,
Shall falter, and fail

Back into the human tongue,
And the dog gets up and goes out
To wander the dawning yard,
I shall crawl to my human bed
And lie there smiling at sunrise,
With the scent of the fox

Burning my brain like an incense,
Floating out of the night wood,
Coming home to my wife and my sons
From the dream of an animal,
Assembling the self I must wake to,
Sleeping to grow back my legs.

DAN

Early May, after cold rain the sun
    baffling cold wind,
Irish setter pup finds a corner near
    the cellar door, all sun and no wind,
Cuddling there he crosses forepaws
    and lays his skull
Sideways on this pillow, dozing in
    a half-sleep,
Browns of hazel nut, mahogany, rosewood,
    played off
              against each other on his paws
              and head.

THE PAW

I return to my limbs with the first
gray light
and here is the gray paw under my hand
the she-wolf Perdita
has come back
to sleep beside me
her spine pressed knuckle to knuckle
down my front
her ears lying against my ribs
on the left side where the heart beats

and she takes its sound for the pulsing
of her paws
we are coursing the black sierra once more
in the starlight
oh Perdita

we are racing over the dark auroras
you and I with no shadow
with no shadow
in the same place

so she came back
again in the black hours
running before the open sack

we have run
these hours together

again
there is blood
on the paw under my fingers
flowing
there is blood then
on the black heights again
in her tracks
our tracks
but vanishing like a shadow

and there is blood
against my ribs again
oh Perdita
she is more beautiful after every wound
as though they were stars
I know
how the haunches are hollowed
stretched out in the dark
at full speed like a constellation
I hear
her breath moving on the fields of frost
my measure

I beat faster
her blood wells through my fingers
my eyes shut to see her
again
my way

before the stars fall
and the mountains go out
and the void wakes
and it is day

but we are gone

DOG DREAMING

The paws twitch in a place of chasing
Where the whimper of this seeming-gentle creature
Rings out terrible, chasing tigers. The fields
Are licking like torches, full of running,
Laced odors, bones stalking, tushed leaps.
So little that is tamed, yet so much
That you would find deeply familiar there.
You are there often, your very eyes,
The unfathomable knowledge behind your face,
The mystery of your will, appraising
Such carnage and triumph; standing there
Strange even to yourself, and loved, and only
A sleeping beast knows who you are.

W. S. MERWIN

AS SHE GOES

The dream-twitch, her back leg as if running
Through morning woods, only she is dying,
And in the rhythm of each breath unsure

Of the last, her whiskers crushed
Against the green of my old coat, the slow
Deliberate words I had learned to use—

But I cannot move; I wait for any sign
Of forgiveness. Instead, a precise
Tremble of her body as it travels

Through fear, her ear fixed to the ground
As if to some other voice. Instead
That moment she lifts her head, turns back

And looks direct into my eye, looking
For herself, to see what it is I see.

HARK, HARK,
HEAR THEM BARK

BARKING DOGS IN THE SNOW

Barking dogs in the snow! Good weather is coming!
Good weather is coming to barking dogs in the snow.
A man changes only slowly. And winter is not yet past.
Bark, dogs, and fill the valleys
Of white with your awful laments.

O HAPPY DOGS OF ENGLAND

O happy dogs of England
Bark well as well you may
if you lived anywhere else
You would not be so gay.

O happy dogs of England
Bark well at errand boys
If you lived anywhere else
You would not be allowed to make such an infernal noise.

THE RAPE OF CHANTICLEER

The silly widow and her daughters two,
Herden these hens' cry and maken woe,
And out at the doors starten they anon,
And saw the fox toward the wood is gone,
And bare upon his back the cock away:
They crieden out, "Harow and wa la wa!
A ha the fox!" and after him they ran,
And eke with staves many another man;
Ran Colle our dog, and Talbot, and Gerland,
And Malkin with her distaff in her hand;
Ran cow and calf, and eke the very hogs,
So fearèd were for barking of the dogs.

THESEUS AND HIPPOLYTA
From A Midsummer Night's Dream

THESEUS:

Go, one of you, find out the forester;
For now our observation is perform'd;
And since we have the vaward of the day,
My love shall hear the music of my hounds.
Uncouple in the western valley; let them go:
Dispatch, I say, and find the forester.
We will, fair queen, up to the mountain's top,
And mark the musical confusion
Of hounds and echo in conjunction.

HIPPOLYTA:

I was with Hercules and Cadmus once,
When in a wood of Crete they bay'd the bear
With hounds of Sparta: never did I hear
Such gallant chiding; for, besides the groves,
The skies, the fountains, every region near
Seem'd all one mutual cry: I never heard
So musical a discord, such sweet thunder.

THESEUS:

My hounds are bred out of the Spartan kind,
So flew'd, so sanded; and their heads are hung
With ears that sweep away the morning dew;

Crook-knee'd, and dew-lapp'd like Thessalian bulls;
Slow in pursuit, but match'd in mouth like bells,
Each under each. A cry more tuneable
Was never holla'd to, nor cheer'd with horn,
In Crete, in Sparta, nor in Thessaly:
Judge when you hear.

WILLIAM SHAKESPEARE

DOG AT NIGHT

At first he stirs uneasily in sleep
And, since the moon does not run off, unfolds
Protesting paws. Grumbling that he must keep
Both eyes awake, he whimpers; then he scolds
And, rising to his feet, demands to know
The stranger's business. You who break the dark
With insolent light, who are you? Where do you go?
But nothing answers his indignant bark.
The moon ignores him, walking on as though
Dogs never were. Stiffened to fury now,
His small hairs stand upright, his howls come fast,
And terrible to hear is the bow-wow
That tears the night. Stirred by this bugle-blast,
The farmer's bitch grows active; without pause
Summons her mastiff and the hound that lies
Three fields away to rally to the cause.
And the next county wakes. And miles beyond
Throats tear themselves and brassy lungs respond
With threats, entreaties, bellowings and cries,
Chasing the white intruder down the skies.

THE BATTLE OF THE PEKES AND THE POLLICLES, AND THE INTERVENTION OF THE GREAT RUMPUSCAT

The Pekes and the Pollicles, everyone knows,
Are proud and implacable passionate foes;
It is always the same, wherever one goes.
And the Pugs and the Poms, although most people say
That they do not like fighting, yet once in a way,
They will now and again join in to the fray
And they
   Bark bark bark bark
   Bark bark BARK BARK
 Until you can hear them all over the Park.

Now on the occasion of which I shall speak
Almost nothing had happened for nearly a week
(And that's a long time for a Pol or a Peke).
The big Police Dog was away from his beat—
I don't know the reason, but most people think
He'd slipped into the Wellington Arms for a drink—
And no one at all was about on the street
When a Peke and a Pollicle happened to meet.
They did not advance, or exactly retreat,
But they glared at each other, and scraped their hind
  feet,

And started to
      Bark bark bark bark
      Bark bark BARK BARK
  Until you could hear them all over the Park.

Now the Peke, although people may say what they please,
Is no British dog, but a Heathen Chinese.
And so all the Pekes, when they heard the uproar,
Some came to the window, some came to the door;
There were surely a dozen, more likely a score.
And together they started to grumble and wheeze
In their huffery-snuffery Heathen Chinese.
But a terrible din is what Pollicles like,
For your Pollicle Dog is a dour Yorkshire tyke,
And his braw Scottish cousins are snappers and biters,
And every dog-jack of them notable fighters;
And so they stepped out, with their pipers in order,
Playing When the Blue Bonnets Came Over the Border.
Then the Pugs and the Poms held no longer aloof,
But some from the balcony, some from the roof,
Joined in
To the din
With a
      Bark bark bark bark
      Bark bark BARK BARK
  Until you could hear them all over the Park.

Now when these bold heroes together assembled,
The traffic all stopped, and the Underground trembled,
And some of the neighbours were so much afraid
That they started to ring up the Fire Brigade.
When suddenly, up from a small basement flat,
Why who should stalk out but the GREAT RUMPUSCAT.
His eyes were like fireballs fearfully blazing,
He gave a great yawn, and his jaws were amazing;
And when he looked out through the bars of the area,
You never saw anything fiercer or hairier.
And what with the glare of his eyes and his yawning,
The Pekes and the Pollicles quickly took warning.
He looked at the sky and he gave a great leap—
And they every last one of them scattered like sheep.

And when the Police Dog returned to his beat,
There wasn't a single one left in the street.

A FRIENDLY WELCOME

'Tis sweet to hear the watch-dog's honest bark
Bay deep-mouthed welcome as we draw near home;
'Tis sweet to know there is an eye will mark
Our coming, and look brighter when we come.

THE THRILL OF
THE HUNT

ON A SPANIEL CALLED BEAU
Killing a Young Bird

A Spaniel, Beau, that fares like you,
    Well-fed, and at his ease,
Should wiser be, than to pursue
    Each trifle that he sees.

But you have kill'd a tiny bird,
    Which flew not till to-day,
Against my orders, whom you heard
    Forbidding you the prey.

Nor did you kill, what you might eat,
    And ease a doggish pain,
For him, though chas'd with furious heat,
    You left where he was slain.

Nor was he of the thievish sort,
    Or one whom blood allures,
But innocent was all his sport,
    Whom you have torn for yours.

My dog! what remedy remains,
    Since, teach you all I can,
I see you, after all my pains,
    So much resemble man!

WILLIAM COWPER

BULL-BAITING

A yet ignobler band is guarded round
    With dogs of war—the spurning bull their prize;
And now he bellows, humbled to the ground,
    And now they sprawl in howlings to the skies.

SHEPHEARD'S DOGGE

From The Shepheardes Calendar, *September*

Thilk same Shepheard mought I well marke;
He has a dogge to byte or to barke;
Never had shepheard so kene a kurre,
That waketh and if but a leafe sturre.
Whilome there wonned a wicked wolfe,
That with many a lambe had glutted his gulfe.
And ever at night wont to repayre
Unto the flocke, when the welkin shone faire,
Ycladde in clothing of seely sheepe,
When the good old man used to sleepe.
Tho at midnight he would barke and ball,
(For he had eft learned a curres call,)
As if a woolfe were emong the sheepe.
With that the shepheard would breake his sleepe,
And send out Lowder (for so his dog hote)
To raunge the fields with wide open throte.
Tho, whenas Lowder was farre awaye,
This wolvish sheepe would catchen his pray . . .
At end, the shepheard his practise spyed,
(For Roffy is wise, and as Argus eyed)
And when at even he came to the flocke,
Fast in theyr folds he did them locke, . . .
For it was a perilous beast above all,
And eke had he cond the shepherds call,

And oft in the night came to the shepecote,
And called Lowder, with a hollow throte,
As if it the old man selfe had bene.
The dog his maisters voice did it weene,
Yet halfe in doubt he opened the dore,
And ranne out, as he was wont of yore.
No sooner was out, but swifter than thought,
Fast by the hyde the wolfe Lowder caught;
And had not Roffy renne to the steven,
Lowder had be slaine thilke same even.

THE FAWNING WHELP

The master Hunt, anon, foot-hot,
With his horn blew three mote
At the uncoupling of his houndis;
Within a while the hart found is,
Y-halloaed, and rechasèd fast
Long time, and so, at the last,
This hart roused and stole away
From all the hounds a privy way.
The hounds had overshot him all,
And were upon a default y-fall,
Therewith the Hunt wonder fast
Blew a forlorn at the last;
I was go walkèd from my tree,
And, as I went, there came by me
A whelp, that fawned me as I stood,
That had y-followed, and could no good;
It came and crept to me as low
Right as it had me y-know,
Held down his head, and joined his ears,
And laid all smooth down his hairs:
I would have caught it anon,
It fled, and was from me gone.

SMALL POEM ABOUT THE HOUNDS
AND THE HARES

After the kill, there is the feast.
And toward the end, when the dancing subsides
and the young have sneaked off somewhere,
the hounds, drunk on the blood of the hares,
begin to talk of how soft
were their pelts, how graceful their leaps,
how lovely their scared, gentle eyes.

INCIDENT
Characteristic of a favourite dog

On his morning rounds the Master
Goes to learn how all things fare;
Searches pasture after pasture,
Sheep and cattle eyes with care;
And, for silence or for talk,
He hath comrades in his walk;
Four dogs, each pair of different breed,
Distinguished two for scent, and two for speed.

See a hare before him started!
—Off they fly in earnest chase;
Every dog is eager-hearted,
All the four are in the race:
And the hare whom they pursue,
Knows from instinct what to do;
Her hope is near: no turn she makes;
But, like an arrow, to the river takes.

Deep the river was, and crusted
Thinly by a one night's frost;
But the nimble Hare hath trusted
To the ice, and safely crost;
She hath crost, and without heed
All are following at full speed,

When, lo! the ice, so thinly spread,
Breaks—and the greyhound, DART, is overhead!

Better fate have PRINCE and SWALLOW—
See them cleaving to the sport!
MUSIC has no heart to follow,
Little MUSIC, she stops short.
She hath neither wish nor heart,
Hers is now another part:
A loving creature she, and brave!
And fondly strives her struggling friend to save.

From the brink her paws she stretches,
Very hands as you would say!
And afflicting moans she fetches,
As he breaks the ice away.
For herself she hath no fears,—
Him alone she sees and hears,—
Makes efforts with complainings; nor gives o'er
Until her fellow sinks to re-appear no more.

THE HUNTING OF THE HARE

Betwixt two ridges of ploughed land lay Wat,
Pressing his body close to earth lay squat.
His nose upon his two forefeet close lies,
Glaring obliquely with his great grey eyes.
His head he always sets against the wind:
If turn his tail, his hairs blow up behind,
Which he too cold will grow; but he is wise,
And keeps his coat still down, so warm he lies.
Thus resting all the day, till sun doth set,
Then riseth up, his relief for to get,
Walking about until the sun doth rise;
Then back returns, down in his form he lies.
At last poor Wat was found, as he there lay,
By huntsmen with their dogs which came that way.
Seeing, gets up, and fast begins to run,
Hoping some ways the cruel dogs to shun.
But they by nature have so quick a scent
That by their nose they trace what way he went;

*   *   *

Into a great thick wood he straightway gets,
Where underneath a broken bough he sits;
At every leaf that with the wind did shake
Did bring such terror, made his heart to ache.
That place he left; to champian plains he went,
Winding about, for to deceive their scent,

And while they snuffling were, to find his track,
Poor Wat, being weary, his swift pace did slack.
On his two hinder legs for ease did sit:
His forefeet rubbed his face from dust and sweat.
Licking his feet, he wiped his ears so clean
That none could tell that Wat had hunted been.
But casting round about his fair great eyes,
The hounds in full career he near him spies;
To Wat it was so terrible a sight,
Fear gave him wings, and made his body light.

* * *

The great slow hounds, their throats did set a base,
The fleet swift hounds as tenors next in place;
The little beagles they a treble sing,
And through the air their voice a round did ring;
Which made a consort as they ran along:
If they but words could speak, might sing a song:
The horns kept time, the hunters shout for joy,
And valiant seem, poor Wat for to destroy.
Spurring their horses to a full career,
Swim rivers deep, leap ditches without fear;
Endanger life and limbs, so fast will ride,
Only to see how patiently Wat died.
For why, the dogs so near his heels did get
That they their sharp teeth in his breech did set.
Then tumbling down, did fall with weeping eyes,
Gives up his ghost, and thus poor Wat he dies.

IT'S A
DOG'S LIFE

APRÈS LA POLITIQUE, LA HAINE
DES BOURBONS

Count Flanders
Was eaten up with pride;
His dog Sanders
Thought only of his inside.

They were a precious couple,
And let the people feed on straw and rubble.

Bitter was the weather,
Bitter the people,
When they flung Count Flanders
From the church steeple.
Bitter was the weather,
Iron the ground,
When Dog Sanders died of a stomach wound.

STEVIE SMITH   149

LAUNCE'S DOG, CRAB
From The Two Gentlemen of Verona

LAUNCE: When a man's servant shall play the cur with
him, look you, it goes hard: one that I brought up of a
puppy; one that I saved from drowning, when three or
four of his blind brothers and sisters went to it! I have
taught him, even as one would say precisely, "thus
I would teach a dog." I was sent to deliver him as a
present to Mistress Silvia from my master; and I came
no sooner into the dining-chamber, but he steps me to
her trencher, and steals her capon's leg: O, 'tis a foul
thing when a cur cannot keep himself in all companies!
I would have, as one should say, one that takes upon
him to be a dog indeed, to be, as it were, a dog at all
things. If I had not had more wit than he, to take a fault
upon me that he did, I think verily he had been hanged
for't; sure as I live, he had suffered for't: you shall
judge. He thrusts me himself into the company of three
or four gentlemanlike dogs, under the duke's table: he
had not been there—bless the mark—a pissing while,
but all the chamber smelt him. "Out with the dog!" says
one: "What cur is that?" says another: "Whip him out,"
says the third: "Hang him up," says the duke. I, having
been acquainted with the smell before, knew it was
Crab, and goes me to the fellow that whips the dogs:
"Friend," quoth I, "you mean to whip the dog?"

"Ay, marry, do I," quoth he. "You do him the more wrong," quoth I; "'twas I did the thing you wot of." He makes me no more ado, but whips me out of the chamber. How many masters would do this for his servant? Nay, I'll be sworn, I have sat in the stocks for puddings he hath stolen, otherwise he had been executed; I have stood on the pillory for geese he hath killed, otherwise he had suffered for 't. Thou thinkest not of this now. Nay, I remember the trick you served me when I took my leave of Madam Silvia: did not I bid thee still mark me, and do as I do? when didst thou see me heave up my leg, and make water against a gentlewoman's farthingale? didst thou ever see me do such a trick?

FULL OF THE MOON

It's full of the moon
The dogs dance out
Through brush and bush and bramble.
They howl and yowl
And growl and prowl.
They amble, ramble, scramble.
They rush through brush.
They push through bush.
They yip and yap and hurr.
They lark around and bark around
With prickles in their fur.
They two-step in the meadow.
They polka on the lawn.
Tonight's the night
The dogs dance out
And chase their tails till dawn.

DOG

He does not look fierce at all, propped scarcely erect
On skinny forelegs in the dust in the glare
In the dog-day heat, the small brown pariah at the edge
Of the shimmering vista of emptiness
Unbroken by any shade and seeming too permanent
To be of any day the afternoon.
Under the sky no color or rather
The natural beige, dust-color, merely
A brighter glare than the ground, beginning
Where the dust does not leave off, and rising
Through the shining distance that weighs and waves
Like water he does not have the air at all
Of vigilance: hindquarters collapsed
Under him like a rag lying shapeless
In the shrunk puddle of his shadow, coat
Caked and staring, hangdog head
That his shoulders can hardly hold up from the dust
And from it dangling the faded tongue, the one
Color to be seen. *Cave canem*; beware
The dog. But he squats harmless,
At his wildest, it might be, wishing that the feeble
Green cast the glare gives to his shadow
Could be green in truth, or be at least a wider
Shadow of some true green; and though he is
Free not tethered (but what in this place

Could one be free of if not the place) surely
He would never attack, nor move except perhaps,
Startled, to flee; surely those dirty tufts
Of coarse hair at his shoulders could never rise
Hostile in hackles, and he has forgotten
Long since the wish to growl; or if he should bare
His teeth it would not be with a lifting
Of lips but with a letting-fall, as it is
With the grins of the dead. And indeed what is there
    here
That he might keep watch over? The dust? The empty
Distance, the insufferable light losing itself
In its own glare? Whatever he was to guard
Is gone. Besides, his glazed eyes
Fixed heavily ahead stare beyond you
Noticing nothing; he does not see you. But wrong:
Look again: it is through you
That he looks, and the danger of his eyes
Is that in them you are not there. He guards indeed
What is gone, what is gone, what has left not so much
As a bone before him, which vigilance needs
No fierceness, and his weariness is not
From the length of his watch, which is endless,
But because nothing, not the weight of days
Not hope, the canicular heat, the dust, nor the mortal
Sky, is to be borne. Approach
If you dare, but doing so you take

In your hands what life is yours, which is less
Than you suppose, for he guards all that is gone,
And even the shimmer of the heated present,
Of the moment before him in which you stand
Is a ghost's shimmer, its past gone out of it, biding
But momently his vigil. Walk past him
If you please, unmolested, but behind his eyes
You will be seen not to be there, in the glaring
Uncharactered reaches of oblivion, and guarded
With the rest of vacancy. Better turn from him
Now when you can and pray that the dust you stand in
And your other darlings be delivered
From the vain distance he is the power of.

PINK DOG
Rio de Janeiro

The sun is blazing and the sky is blue.
Umbrellas clothe the beach in every hue.
Naked, you trot across the avenue.

Oh, never have I seen a dog so bare!
Naked and pink, without a single hair . . .
Startled, the passersby draw back and stare.

Of course they're mortally afraid of rabies.
You are not mad; you have a case of scabies
but look intelligent. Where are your babies?

(A nursing mother, by those hanging teats.)
In what slum have you hidden them, poor bitch,
while you go begging, living by your wits?

Didn't you know? It's been in all the papers,
to solve this problem, how they deal with beggars?
They take and throw them in the tidal rivers.

Yes, idiots, paralytic, parasites
go bobbing in the ebbing sewage, nights
out in the suburbs, where there are no lights.

If they do this to anyone who begs,
drugged, drunk, or sober, with or without legs,
what would they do to sick, four-leggèd dogs?

In the cafés and on the sidewalk corners
the joke is going round that all the beggars
who can afford them now wear life preservers.

In your condition you would not be able
even to float, much less to dog-paddle.
Now look, the practical, the sensible

solution is to wear a *fantasía*.
Tonight you simply can't afford to be an
eyesore. But no one will ever see a

dog in *máscara* this time of year.
Ash Wednesday'll come but Carnival is here.
What sambas can you dance? What will you wear?

They say that Carnival's degenerating
—radios, Americans, or something,
have ruined it completely. They're just talking.

Carnival is always wonderful!
A depilated dog would not look well.
Dress up! Dress up and dance at Carnival!

DOG PROSPECTUS

The dog must see your corpse. The last thing that
    you feel
Must be the dog's warm-tufa licking of your hand,
Its clear gaze on your trembling lips, then
Snapping at flies, catches the last breath in its teeth,
And trots off with you quickly to the Judge,
Your advocate and friend. The corpse a dog has
    not seen
Pollutes a thousand men; the Bishop's hound
Tucked like a cushion at his tombstone feet
Once through the door carries a helix staff
And looks like Hermes on that side, the Bishop
    tumbling
On the puppy-paws of death . . .
            as a temporary Professor at this U
I practise, when the campus swarms with them,
Focusing out the students, so the place
Is amply empty, except for a few dogs.
They should study here, the U enrol them
And take more fees, at agreed standards teaching
Elementary Urinology, and Advanced
Arboreal Urinology: The Seasons and their Smells;
Freshman Osteology: The Selection and Concealment
Of Bones; Janitology: The Budding Watchdog, with
Fawning, a two-semester course. Lunar Vocalization,

Or Baying at the Moon; the "lame-dog bid for
    sympathy
With big sad eyes and hanging tongue", which is
Cosmetic Ophthalmology with Intermittent
    Claudication
In the Rhetorical Physiognomy Gym. Shit and Its
    Meaning;
Coprology: the Dog-Turd and Modern Legislation;
    The
Eating of Jezebel, or Abreactive Phantasising; The
    Black Dog,
Or Studies in Melancholy; The Age of Worry:
An Era Favourable to Dogs . . . How to Beg:
A Long-Term Economic Good; with How to Fuck,
Or Staggering in Six-Legged Joy; Fleas,
A Useful Oracle, and in this same last year
The Dedicated Castrate or God's Eunuch,
The Canine Celibate as Almost-Man;
And finally how, if uncastrated,
To change places and become Master-Dog,
The Palindromic Homocane and Goddog-Doggod,
Wise Hermes of the Intelligent Nose,

Leading to the Degree of Master of Hounds.
The campus throngs with hounds, this degree

Is very popular, alas—
I focus them out: in ample emptiness
A few humans hurry to their deep study
Without prospectus, without University.
This one is desirous of becoming a perfect scribe:
He knows vigilance, ferocity, and how to bark;
This one studies gazing as the dogs used to
On the images of the gods, as prophets should.
What gods, what images?

Those glorious trees, trilling with birds, cicadas,
Pillars of the sky, our books and ancestors;
I piss my tribute here, I cannot help it;
The few humans left, noble as dogs once were,
Piss on this university.

HOPE

At the foot of the stairs
my black dog sits;
in his body,
out of his wits.

On the other side
of the shut front door
there's a female dog
he's nervous for.

She's the whole size
of his mind—immense.
Hope ruling him
past sense.

WILLIAM DICKEY

EATING POETRY

Ink runs from the corners of my mouth.
There is no happiness like mine.
I have been eating poetry.

The librarian does not believe what she sees.
Her eyes are sad
and she walks with her hands in her dress.

The poems are gone.
The light is dim.
The dogs are on the basement stairs and coming up.

Their eyeballs roll,
their blond legs burn like brush.
The poor librarian begins to stamp her feet and weep.
She does not understand.
When I get on my knees and lick her hand,
she screams.

I am a new man.
I snarl at her and bark.
I romp with joy in the bookish dark.

TWO DOGS

Enchantment creek underbank pollen, are the stiff
    scents he makes,
hot grass rolling and rabbit-dig but only saliva
    chickweed.
Road pizza clay bird, hers answer him, rot-spiced good.
    Blachy grass,
she adds, ant log in hot sunshine. Snake two sunups
    back. Orifice?
Orifice, he wriggles. Night fox? Night fox, with left
    pad wound.
Cement bag, hints his shoulder. Cat meat, boasts his
    tail, twice enjoyed.
Folded sapless inside me, she clenches. He retracts
    initial blood.
Frosty darks coming, he nuzzles. High wind rock
    human-free howl,
her different law. Soon. Away, away, eucalypts
    speeding—
Bark! I water for it. Her eyes go binocular, as in pawed
hop frog snack play. Come ploughed, she jumps
    ground. Bark tractor,
white bitterhead grub and pull scarecrow. Me! Assents
    his urine.

THE UNRULY THOUGHTS OF THE
DOG TRAINER'S LOVER

Into the wheat-thrown fields we lead
the leashed dogs, the well-trained hounds;
they leap to mind through the weedy
Queen Anne's lace. He orders them, "Circle round,
round." I'm a willing believer.

They run together—gray water, tail to mouth—
in wheeling stories. Their frilled jaws
can hold eggs, live rabbits, our wrists. At his brief sign
they make no sound. I am properly awed.
Their paws wear great rings of grass down.

He wields the commands "Sit," "Stay"
like a stick and a thorn. He can say "Fetch" or "Leave":
they scatter in ashen explosions. Waving
devoted tails like prayer flags, they look for reprieve
    to me.
I shrug. He gestures "Heel." They come through
    meticulous paces.

I'm here to reward us all when we lie down,
to roll over into the pasture hay, to carry a sack
of marrow bones tight in my loose
hand. I wear his clothes like khaki
fatigues in the afternoon. He stands his ground.

I hear mongrel packs have taken the roads upstate,
attacking deer at will. But we will go to the kennel
      show
for blue, snapping ribbons. The fairgrounds will shake
under the truck. He'll call the dogs: "Go slowly,
      hounds.
I said go slow." We all may have made a grave mistake.

DOG

The dog trots freely in the street
and sees reality
and the things he sees
are bigger than himself
and the things he sees
are his reality
Drunks in doorways
Moons on trees
The dog trots freely thru the streets
and the things he sees
are smaller than himself
Fish on newsprint
Ants in holes
Chickens in Chinatown windows
their heads a block away
The dog trots freely in the street
and the things he smells
smell something like himself
The dog trots freely in the streets
past puddles and babies
cats and cigars
poolrooms and policemen
He doesn't hate cops
He merely has no use for them
and he goes past them

166

and past the dead cows hung up whole
in front of the San Francisco Meat Market
He would rather eat a tender cow
than a tough policeman
though either might do
And he goes past the Romeo Ravioli Factory
and past Coit's Tower
but he's not afraid of Congressman Doyle
although what he hears is very discouraging
very depressing
very absurd
to a sad young dog like himself
to a serious dog like himself
But he has his own free world to live in
His own fleas to eat
He will not be muzzled
Congressman Doyle is just another
fire hydrant
to him
The dog trots freely in the street
and has his own dog's life to live
and to think about
and to reflect upon
touching and tasting and testing everything
investigating everything

without benefit of perjury
a real realist
with a real tale to tell
and a real tail to tell it with
a real live
          barking
                    democratic dog
engaging in real
                    free enterprise
with something to say
                    about ontology
something to say
          about reality
                    and how to see it
                              and how to hear it
with his head cocked sideways
                    at streetcorners
as if he is just about to have
                    his picture taken
                              for Victor Records
          listening for
                    His Master's Voice
          and looking
                    like a living questionmark
                    into the
                    great gramophone
                    of puzzling existence

with its wondrous hollow horn
    which always seems
just about to spout forth
                some Victorious answer
            to everything

THE TOY BONE

Looking through boxes
in the attic of my mother's house in Hamden,
I find a model airplane, snapshots
of a dog wearing baby clothes,
a catcher's mitt—the oiled
pocket eaten
by mice—and I discover
the toy bone.

I sat alone each day
after school, in the living room
of my parents' house in Hamden, ten
years old, eating
slices of plain white bread.
I listened to the record, Connie
Boswell singing
again and again, her voice
turning like a heel, "The Kerry Dancers,"
and I knew she was crippled, and sang
from a wheelchair. I played
with Zippy, my red and white
Shetland collie, throwing
his toy bone
into the air and catching it, or letting it fall,

while he watched me
with intent, curious eyes.

I was happy
in the room dark with the shades drawn.

SCROPPO'S DOG

In the early morning, past the shut houses,
past the harbor shut in fog, I walk free and
single. It is summer—that's lucky. The whole
day is mine. At the end of our village I stop
to greet Scroppo's dog, whose chain is wrapped
around a large dusty boulder. His black coat
is gray, from crouching every day in the gravel
of Scroppo's yard—a yard by a scrap-filled pond,
where Scroppo deals in wrecked cars and car parts.
I guess he gets them from crashes on the expressway,
or from abandoned junks he loots by the roadside.

I don't know the name of Scroppo's dog. I remember
him, years ago, as a big fierce-looking pup.
It may have been his first day chained there,
or shortly after, that he first greeted me:
his eyes big nuggets shooting orange sparks, his
red tongue rippling out between clean fangs—
fangs as white as lilies of the valley that bloom
in a leafy border by Scroppo's weathered porch.
It was late May, as now, when with sudden joyful
bark, black fur erect and gleaming, the dog
rushed toward me—but was stopped by his chain,
a chain then bright and new. I would have met
and stroked him, but didn't dare get near him,

in his strangled frenzy—in his unbelief—
that something at his throat cut short
his coming, going, leaping, circling, running—
something he couldn't bite through, tripped him:
he could go only so far: to the trash in the weeds
at the end of the driveway, to the edge
of the oily, broken cement in back, where Scroppo's
muddy flatbed truck stands at night.

Now, as I walk toward him, the dog growls,
then cowers back. He is old and fat and dirty,
and his eyes spit equal hate and fear.
He knows exactly how far he can strain
from the rock and the wrapped chain. There's
a trench in a circle in the oily dirt his paws
have dug. Days and weeks and months and years
of summer heat and winter cold have been survived
within the radius of that chain.
Scroppo's dog knows me, and wants to come and
touch. At the same time, his duty to expel
the intruder makes him bare his teeth and
bristle. He pounds his matted tail, he snarls
while cringing, alternately stretches toward me
and springs back. His bark, husky and cracked,
follows me for a block, until I turn the corner,
crossing the boundary of the cove.

I've never touched Scroppo's dog, and his
yearning tongue has never licked me. Yet, we
know each other well. Subject to the seasons'
extremes, confined to the limits of our yard,
early fettered by an obscure master in whose
power we bask, bones grow frail while steel
thickens; while rock fattens, passions and
senses pale. Scroppo's dog sniffs dust.
He sleeps a lot. My nose grown blunt, I need
to remember the salty damp of the air's taste
on summer mornings, first snowfall's freshness,
the smoke of burning leaves. Each midday,
when the firehouse whistle blows, a duet
of keen, weird howls is heard, as, at the steep
edge of hopelessness, with muzzle pointed,
ears flat, eyes shut, Scroppo's dog forlornly
yodels in time to the village siren sounding noon.

LONE DOG

I'm a lean dog, a keen dog, a wild dog, and lone;
I'm a rough dog, a tough dog, hunting on my own;
I'm a bad dog, a mad dog, teasing silly sheep;
I love to sit and bay the moon, to keep fat souls from sleep.

I'll never be a lap dog, licking dirty feet,
A sleek dog, a meek dog, cringing for my meat,
Not for me the fireside, the well-filled plate,
But shut door, and sharp stone, and cuff and kick and hate.

Not for me the other dogs, running by my side,
Some have run a short while, but none of them would
     bide.
O mine is still the lone trail, the hard trail, the best,
Wide wind, and wild stars, and hunger of the quest!

IRENE RUTHERFORD McLEOD   175

WHAT THE DOG PERHAPS HEARS

If an inaudible whistle
blown between our lips
can send him home to us,
then silence is perhaps
the sound of spiders breathing
and roots mining the earth;
it may be asparagus heaving,
headfirst, into the light
and the long brown sound
of cracked cups, when it happens.
We would like to ask the dog
if there is a continuous whir
because the child in the house
keeps growing, if the snake
really stretches full length
without a click and the sun
breaks through clouds without
a decibel of effort,
whether in autumn, when the trees
dry up their wells, there isn't a shudder
too high for us to hear.

What is it like up there
above the shut-off level
of our simple ears?

176

For us there was no birth cry,
the newborn bird is suddenly here,
the egg broken, the nest alive,
and we heard nothing when the world changed.

DOG

I can hear him out in the kitchen,
his lapping the night's only music,
head bowed over the waterbowl
like an illustration in a book for boys.

He enters the room with such etiquette,
licking my bare ankle as if he understood
the Braille of the skin.

Then he makes three circles around himself,
flattening his ancient memory of tall grass
before dropping his weight with a sigh on the floor.

This is the spot where he will spend the night,
his ears listening for the syllable of his name,
his tongue hidden in his long mouth
like a strange naked hermit in a cave.

POWER SOURCE

Like harnessing
the tides or the wind,
how about attaching
dogs' tails
to power generators?

I want the job
of patting the dog
to keep its tail
wagging.

Dogs could generate
enough electricity
for cities, for countries—
light up the world!

THE SONG OF THE MISCHIEVOUS DOG
Written at the age of 11

There are many who say that a dog has his day,
And a cat has a number of lives;
There are others who think that a lobster is pink,
And that bees never work in their hives.
There are fewer, of course, who insist that a horse
Has a horn and two humps on its head,
And a fellow who jests that a mare can build nests
Is as rare as a donkey that's red.
Yet in spite of all this, I have moments of bliss,
For I cherish a passion for bones,
And though doubtful of biscuit, I'm willing to risk it,
And love to chase rabbits and stones.
But my greatest delight is to take a good bite
At a calf that is plump and delicious;
And if I indulge in a bite at a bulge,
Let's hope you won't think me too vicious.

DOGGEREL,
OR, IN THEIR
OWN WORDS

CONFESSION OF A GLUTTON

after i ate my dinner then i ate
part of a shoe
i found some archies by a bathroom pipe
and ate them too
i ate some glue
i ate a bone that had got nice and ripe
six weeks buried in the ground
i ate a little mousie that i found
i ate some sawdust from the cellar floor
it tasted sweet
i ate some outcast meat
and some roach paste by the pantry door
and then the missis had some folks to tea
nice folks who petted me
and so i ate
cakes from a plate
i ate some polish that they use
for boots and shoes
and then i went back to the missis swell tea party
i guess i must have eat too hearty
of something maybe cake
for then came the earthquake
you should have seen the missis face
and when the boss came in she said
no wonder that dog hangs his head

he knows hes in disgrace
i am a well intentioned little pup
but sometimes things come up
to get a little dog in bad
and now i feel so very very sad
but the boss said never mind old scout
time wears disgraces out

A POPULAR PERSONAGE AT HOME

"I live here: 'Wessex' is my name:
I am a dog known rather well:
I guard the house; but how that came
To be my whim I cannot tell.

"With a leap and a heart elate I go
At the end of an hour's expectancy
To take a walk of a mile or so
With the folk I let live here with me.

"Along the path, amid the grass
I sniff, and find out rarest smells
For rolling over as I pass
The open fields towards the dells.

"No doubt I shall always cross this sill,
And turn the corner, and stand steady,
Gazing back for my mistress till
She reaches where I have run already,

"And that this meadow with its brook,
And bulrush, even as it appears
As I plunge by with hasty look,
Will stay the same a thousand years."

Thus "Wessex". But a dubious ray
At times informs his steadfast eye,
Just for a trice, as though to say,
"Yet, will this pass, and pass shall I?"

ON THE COLLAR OF TIGER

Pray steal me not; I'm Mrs Dingley's,
Whose heart in this four-footed thing lies.

ENGRAVED ON THE COLLAR OF A DOG, WHICH I GAVE TO HIS ROYAL HIGHNESS

I am his Highness' dog at Kew;
Pray tell me, sir, whose dog are you?

MOMMY

You do not do, you do not do
Any more, pig's hoof
On which I have chewed like a rat
For six hours in the dark
Barely daring to breathe or bark.

Mommy, I have had to feed myself
You didn't come home in time
Plastic heavy, a bag full of garbage
Ghastly leftovers with one meatless bone
Ach, woof.

A car, a car
Chugging me off like a dog
A dog to the cleaners, the vet
I begin to talk like a dog
I think I may well be a dog.

Not God but God spelled backwards
So tiny any shoe could squash me
Every puppy loves a dominatrix
The boot on the paw, the brutess
Lick the boot of a brute like you.

Mommy, I bit your pretty red cushion in two
I was hungry when you left at three
At five, I tried to claw through the door
And get back, back, back to you.
I knew garbage bones wouldn't do.

So mommy, I'm finally through
The black answering machine's been chewed off at
    the wire
The messages can't worm through.

CONTENTMENT

I like the way that the world is made,
    (Tickle me, please, behind the ears)
With part in the sun and part in the shade
    (Tickle me, *please*, behind the ears).
This comfortable spot beneath a tree
Was probably planned for you and me;
Why *do* you suppose God made a flea?
    Tickle me more behind the ears.

I hear a cricket or some such bug
    (Tickle me, please, behind the ears)
And there is a hole some creature dug
    (Tickle me, *please*, behind the ears).
I can't quite smell it from where we sit,
But I think a rabbit would hardly fit;
Tomorrow, perhaps, I'll look into it:
    Tickle me more behind the ears.

A troublesome fly is near my nose,
    (Tickle me, please, behind the ears);
He thinks I'll snap at him, I suppose,
    (Tickle me, *please*, behind the ears).
If I lay on my back with my legs in air
Would you scratch my stomach, just here and there?
It's a puppy trick and I don't much care,
    But tickle me more behind the ears.

Heaven, I guess, is all like this
    (Tickle me, please, behind the ears);
It's my idea of eternal bliss
    (Tickle me, *please*, behind the ears).
With angel cats for a dog to chase,
And a very extensive barking space,
And big bones buried all over the place,—
    And you, to tickle behind my ears.

YOKO

All today I lie in the bottom of the wardrobe
feeling low but sometimes getting up
to moodily lumber across rooms
and lap from the toilet bowl, it is so sultry
and then I hear the noise of firecrackers again
all New York is jaggedy with firecrackers today
and I go back to the wardrobe gloomy
trying to void my mind of them.
I am confused, I feel loose and unfitted.

At last deep in the stairwell I hear a tread,
it is him, my leader, my love.
I run to the door and listen to his approach.
Now I can smell him, what a good man he is,
I love it when he has the sweat of work on him,
as he enters I yodel with happiness,
I throw my body up against his, I try to lick his lips,
I care about him more than anything.

After we eat we go for a walk to the piers.
I leap into the standing warmth, I plunge into
the combination of old and new smells.
Here on a garbage can at the bottom, so interesting,
what sister or brother I wonder left this message
     I sniff.

I too piss there, and go on.
Here a hydrant there a pole
here's a smell I left yesterday, well that's disappointing
but I piss there anyway, and go on.

I investigate so much that in the end
it is for form's sake only, only a drop comes out.

I investigate tar and rotten sandwiches, everything,
      and go on.

And here a dried old turd, so interesting
so old, so dry, yet so subtle and mellow.
I can place it finely, I really appreciate it,
a gold distant smell like packed autumn leaves in
      winter
reminding me how what is rich and fierce when
      excreted
becomes weathered and mild
                              but always interesting
and reminding me of what I have to do.

My leader looks on and expresses his approval.

I sniff it well and later I sniff the air well
a wind is meeting us after the close July day
rain is getting near too but first the wind.

Joy, joy,
being outside with you, active, investigating it all,
with bowels emptied, feeling your approval
and then running on, the big fleet Yoko,
my body in its excellent black coat never lets me down,
returning to you (as I always will, you know that)
and now
              filling myself out with myself, no longer
                    confused,
my panting pushing apart my black lips, but unmoving,
I stand with you braced against the wind.

THOM GUNN   195

THE BLOODHOUND SPEAKS

I am the dog world's best detective.
My sleuthing nose is so effective
I sniff the guilty at a distance
And then they lead a doomed existence.
My well-known record for convictions
Has earned me lots of maledictions
From those whose trail of crime I scented
And sent to prison, unlamented.
Folks either must avoid temptation
Or face my nasal accusation.

A DOG'S EYE VIEW

The people whom I take to walk
    I love and yet deplore,
Such things of real importance
    They persistently ignore.
The sights and smells that thrill me
    They stolidly pass by,
Then stop and stare in rapture
    At nothing in the sky.

They waste such time in stopping
    To look at things like flowers.
They pick the dullest places
    To settle down for hours.
Sometimes I really wonder
    If they can hear and smell;
Such vital things escape them—
    And yet they mean so well!

THE PROMOTION

I was a dog in my former life, a very good dog, and, thus, I was promoted to a human being. I liked being a dog. I worked for a poor farmer, guarding and herding his sheep. Wolves and coyotes tried to get past me almost every night, and not once did I lose a sheep. The farmer rewarded me with good food, food from his table. He may have been poor, but he ate well. And his children played with me, when they weren't in school or working in the field. I had all the love any dog could hope for. When I got old, they got a new dog, and I trained him in the tricks of the trade. He quickly learned, and the farmer brought me into the house to live with the family. I brought the farmer his slippers in the morning, as he was getting old, too. I was dying slowly, a little bit at a time. The farmer knew this and would bring the new dog in to visit me from time to time. The new dog would entertain me with his flips and flops and nuzzles. And then one morning I just didn't get up. They gave me a fine burial down by the stream under a shade tree. That was the end of my being a dog. Sometimes I miss it so I sit by the window and cry. I live in a high-rise that looks out at a bunch of other high-rises.

198

At my job I work in a cubicle and barely speak
to anyone all day. This is my reward for being
a good dog. The human wolves don't even see me.
They fear me not.

HOMER'S SEEING-EYE DOG

Most of the time he wrote, a sort of sleep
with a purpose, so far as I could tell.
How he got from the dark of sleep
to the dark of waking up I'll never know;
the lax sprawl sleep allowed him
began to set from the edges in,
like a custard, and then he was awake—
me too, of course, wriggling my ears
while he unlocked his bladder and stream
of dopey wake-up jokes. The one
about the wine-dark pee I hated instantly.
I stood at the ready, like a god
in an epic, but there was never much
to do. Oh, now and then I'd make a sure
intervention, save a life, whatever.
But my exploits don't interest you,
and of his life all I can say is that
when he'd poured out his work
the best of it was gone and then he died.
He was a great man and I loved him.
Not a whimper about his sex life—
how I detest your prurience—
but here's a farewell literary tip:
I myself am the model for Penelope.
Don't snicker, you hairless moron,

I know so well what "faithful" means
there's not even a word for it in Dog.
I just embody it. I think you bipeds
have a catchphrase for it: "To thine own self
be true, . . ." though like a blind man's shadow,
the second half is only there for those who know
it's missing. Merely a dog, I'll tell you
what it is: ". . . as if you had a choice."

DOG KIBBLE: A VILLANELLE

Life is never meaningless: there is always food.
All day I sit upon the stairs, nose between the bars,
and consider kibble—its smell, its taste, its *mood*—

and I am happy. We walk back to the woods
after lunch (me and the humans) and under leaves
    there are
so many dark crunchy things to eat that I should

not eat but I eat anyway. They are so good!
Even when they make me sick at home or in the car,
I like them. I like to eat. I brood

about the taste of kibble hours before it's chewed.
They keep my meals in the kitchen in a plastic jar.
Don't put me on your couch, please, Dr Freud,

I'm sweet and simple and I'm good.
When I'm sad or sick, not up to par,
I sleep downstairs curled near the toilet. I'm not crude.

I've known shame, and joy, and I have viewed
delicious sights. I don't wander. I don't go far.
Life isn't meaningless because there's food.
Consider kibble: its smell, its taste, its mood.

THE HOUSE DOG'S GRAVE
Haig, an English bulldog

I've changed my ways a little; I cannot now
Run with you in the evenings along the shore,
Except in a kind of dream; and you, if you dream a
      moment,
You see me there.

So leave awhile the paw-marks on the front door
Where I used to scratch to go out or in,
And you'd soon open; leave on the kitchen floor
The marks of my drinking-pan.

I cannot lie by your fire as I used to do
On the warm stone,
Nor at the foot of your bed; no, all the night through
I lie alone.

But your kind thought has laid me less than six feet
Outside your window where firelight so often plays,
And where you sit to read—and I fear often grieving
      for me—
Every night your lamplight lies on my place.

You, man and woman, live so long, it is hard
To think of you ever dying.

A little dog would get tired, living so long.
I hope that when you are lying

Under the ground like me your lives will appear
As good and joyful as mine.
No, dear, that's too much hope: you are not so well
        cared for
As I have been,

And never have known the passionate undivided
Fidelities that I knew.
Your minds are perhaps too active, too many-sided....
But to me you were true.

You were never masters, but friends. I was your friend.
I loved you well, and was loved. Deep love endures
To the end and far past the end. If this is my end,
I am not lonely. I am not afraid. I am still yours.

ORIANE

My name is Oriane,
the lurcher:
half whippet, half border collie,
bred to course
for hares and rabbits
(there are no hares,
only rabbits):
and so I do,
and chase my rubber ball
and play in waves,
and cuddle
in arms that love me.
This is my home:
its name is
                    Oriane

THE SADNESS OF PUPPIES

Up there, squirrels, teasing and clacking.
Birds, up there, away and away.
Up there, plum flowers, petals falling
everywhere too fast.
Down here, my nose can't stop.
My tail nearly levitates my whole behind.
Down here, once in a while, a tongue on kid tongue,
often a tongue on skin the color inside my ear when
        it flaps
open and one of them refolds it,
but no one licks back.
Down here, first teeth drop out on the floor.
Down here, feet I like to lie on, warmer.
Up there, she says, "Puppy love."
Up there, squirrels.

BIRCH

You gonna eat that?
You gonna eat that?
You gonna eat that?

I'll eat that.

IN REMEMBRANCE

EPITAPH TO A DOG

On a monument in the garden of Newstead Abbey

NEAR THIS SPOT
ARE DEPOSITED THE REMAINS
OF ONE
WHO POSSESSED BEAUTY
WITHOUT VANITY,
STRENGTH WITHOUT INSOLENCE,
COURAGE WITHOUT FEROCITY,
AND ALL THE VIRTUES OF MAN
WITHOUT HIS VICES.

THIS PRAISE, WHICH WOULD BE UNMEANING FLATTERY
IF INSCRIBED OVER HUMAN ASHES,
IS BUT A JUST TRIBUTE TO THE MEMORY OF
"BOATSWAIN," A DOG
WHO WAS BORN AT NEWFOUNDLAND,
MAY, 1803,
AND DIED AT NEWSTEAD ABBEY
NOV. 18, 1808

When some proud son of man returns to earth,
Unknown to glory, but upheld by birth,
The sculptor's art exhausts the pomp of woe,
And storied urns record who rests below;
When all is done, upon the tomb is seen,

211

Not what he was, but what he should have been.
But the poor dog, in life the firmest friend,
The first to welcome, foremost to defend,
Whose honest heart is still his master's own,
Who labours, fights, lives, breathes for him alone,
Unhonoured falls, unnoticed all his worth,
Denied in heaven the soul he held on earth—
While man, vain insect! hopes to be forgiven,
And claims himself a sole exclusive heaven.
Oh man! thou feeble tenant of an hour,
Debased by slavery, or corrupt by power—
Who knows thee well must quit thee with disgust,
Degraded mass of animated dust!
Thy love is lust, thy friendship all a cheat,
Thy smiles hypocrisy, thy words deceit!
By nature vile, ennobled but by name,
Each kindred brute might bid thee blush for shame.
Ye, who perchance behold this simple urn,
Pass on—it honours none you wish to mourn.
To mark a friend's remains these stones arise;
I never knew but one—and there he lies.

KAISER DEAD

What, Kaiser dead? The heavy news
Post-haste to Cobham calls the Muse,
From where in Farringford she brews
      The ode sublime,
Or with Pen-bryn's bold bard pursues
      A rival rhyme.

Kai's bracelet tail, Kai's busy feet,
Were known to all the village street.
"What, poor Kai dead?" say all I meet;
      "A loss indeed!"
O for the croon pathetic, sweet,
      Of Robin's reed!

Six years ago I brought him down,
A baby dog, from London town;
Round his small throat of black and brown
      A ribbon blue,
And vouched by glorious renown
      A dachshound true.

His mother, most majestic dame,
Of blood unmixed, from Potsdam came;
And Kaiser's race we deemed the same—
      No lineage higher.

And so he bore the imperial name.
　　　　　But ah, his sire!

Soon, soon the days conviction bring.
The collie hair, the collie swing,
The tail's indomitable ring,
　　　　　The eye's unrest—
The case was clear; a mongrel thing
　　　　　Kai stood confest.

But all those virtues, which commend
The humbler sort who serve and tend,
Were thine in store, thou faithful friend.
　　　　　What sense, what cheer!
To us, declining tow'rds our end,
　　　　　A mate how dear!

　　　　　*　　*　　*

Thine eye was bright, thy coat it shone;
Thou hadst thine errands, off and on;
In joy thy last morn flew; anon,
　　　　　A fit! All's over;
And thou art gone where Geist hath gone,
　　　　　And Toss, and Rover.

GEIST'S GRAVE

Four years! and didst thou stay above
The ground which hides thee now, but four?
And all that life and all that love
Were crowded, Geist, into no more?

Only four years those winning ways,
Which make me for thy presence yearn,
Call'd us to pet thee or to praise,
Dear little friend! at every turn.

That loving heart, that patient soul,
Had they indeed no longer span,
To run their course, and reach their goal,
And read their homily to man?

That liquid, melancholy eye,
From whose pathetic, soul-fed springs
Seem'd surging the Virgilian cry
The sense of tears in mortal things—

That steadfast, mournful strain, consoled
By spirits gloriously gay,
And temper of heroic mould—
What, was four years their whole short day?

Yes, only four!—and not the course
Of all the centuries to come,
And not the infinite resource
Of Nature, with her countless sum

Of figures, with her fulness vast
Of new creation evermore,
Can ever quite repeat the past,
Or just thy little self restore.

Stern law of every mortal lot!
Which man, proud man, finds hard to bear,
And builds himself I know not what
Of second life I know not where.

But thou, when struck, thine hour to go,
On us, who stood despondent by,
A meek last glance of love didst throw,
And humbly lay thee down to die.

Yet would we keep thee in our heart—
Would fix our favourite on the scene,
Nor let thee utterly depart,
And be as if thou ne'er hadst been.

And so there rise these lines of verse
On lips that rarely form them now;

While to each other we rehearse
Such ways, such arts, such looks hadst thou.

We stroke thy broad brown paws again,
We bid thee to thy vacant chair,
We greet thee by the window-pane,
We hear thy scuffle on the stair.

We see the flaps of thy large ears
Quick raised to ask which way we go;
Crossing the frozen lake, appears
Thy small black figure on the snow!

Nor to us only art thou dear
Who mourn thee in thine English home;
Thou hast thine absent master's tear,
Dropt by the far Australian foam.

Thy memory lasts both here and there,
And thou shalt live as long as we.
And after that—thou didst not care!
In us was all the world to thee.

Yet, fondly zealous for thy fame,
Even to a date beyond our own
We strive to carry down thy name,
By mounded turf and graven stone.

We lay thee, close within our reach,
Here, where the grass is smooth and warm,
Between the holly and the beech,
Where oft we watched thy couchant form,

Asleep, yet lending half an ear
To travellers on the Portsmouth road;—
There build we thee, O guardian dear,
Marked with a stone, thy last abode!

Then some, who through this garden pass,
When we too, like thyself, are clay,
Shall see thy grave upon the grass
And stop before the stone and say:

People who lived here long ago
Did by this stone it seems intend
To name for future times to know
The dachshound Geist their little friend.

UPON HIS SPANIEL, TRACIE

Now thou art dead, no eye shall ever see
For shape and service spaniel like to thee.
This shall my love do, give thy sad death one
Tear, that deserves of me a million.

EPITAPH ON FOP

A dog belonging to Lady Throckmorton

Though once a puppy, and though Fop by name,
Here moulders one, whose bones some honour claim;
No sycophant, although of spaniel race!
And though no hound, a martyr to the chase!
Ye squirrels, rabbits, leverets, rejoice!
Your haunts no longer echo to his voice.

This record of his fate exulting view,
He died worn out with vain pursuit of you.
　　"Yes!" the indignant shade of Fop replies,
"And worn with vain pursuit, man also dies."

DEAD DOG

One day I found a lost dog in the street.
The hairs about its grin were spiked with blood,
And it lay still as stone. It must have been
A little dog, for though I only stood
Nine inches for each one of my four years
I picked it up and took it home. My mother
Squealed, and later father spaded out
A bed and tucked my mongrel down in mud.

I can't remember any feeling but
A moderate pity, cool not swollen-eyed;
Almost a godlike feeling now it seems.
My lump of dog was ordinary as bread.
I have no recollection of the school
Where I was taught my terror of the dead.

TALKING TO DOGS
In memoriam Rolfi Strobl. Run over, June 9th, 1970

From us, of course, you want gristly bones
and to be led through exciting odourscapes
 —their colours don't matter—with the chance
of a rabbit to chase or of meeting
 a fellow arse-hole to snuzzle at,
but your deepest fury is to be accepted
 as junior members of a Salon
suaver in taste and manners than a pack,
 to be scratched on the belly and talked to.
Probably, you only hear vowels and then only if
 uttered with lyrical emphasis,
so we cannot tell you a story, even
 when it is true, nor drily dissect
in the third person neighbours who are not there
 or things which can't blush. And what do we,
those of us who are householders, not shepherds
 or killers or polar explorers,
ask from you? The admiration of creatures
 to whom mirrors mean nothing, who never
false your expression and so remind us
 that we as well are still social retards,
who have never learned to command our feelings
 and don't want to, really. Some great men,

Goethe and Lear, for instance, have disliked you,
    which seems eccentric, but good people,
if they keep one, have good dogs. (The reverse
    is not so, for some very bad hats
handle you very well.) It's those who crave
    a querulous permanent baby,
or a little detachable penis,
    who can, and often do, debase you.
Humour and joy to your thinking are one,
    so that you laugh with your whole body,
and nothing dismays you more than the noise
    of our local superior titters.
(But then our young males are dismayed by yours
    to whom, except when a bitch is air-borne,
chastity seems to present no problem.)
    Being quicker to sense unhappiness
without having to be told the dreary
    details or who is to blame, in dark hours
your silence may be of more help than many
    two-legged comforters. In citizens
obedience is not always a virtue,
    but yours need not make us uneasy
because, though child-like, you are complete, no New
    Generation whom it's our duty

to disappoint since, until they notice
      our failings, they will never bother
to make their own mistakes. Let difference
      remain our bond, yes, and the one trait
both have in common, a sense of theatre.

EXEMPLARY NICK

Here lies poor Nick, an honest creature,
Of faithful, gentle, courteous nature;
A parlour pet unspoiled by favour,
A pattern of good dog behaviour.
Without a wish, without a dream,
Beyond his home and friends at Cheam,
Contentedly through life he trotted
Along the path that fate allotted;
Till Time, his aged body wearing,
Bereaved him of his sight and hearing,
Then laid him down without a pain
To sleep, and never wake again.

SYDNEY SMITH

RUBY

Accidentally shot, November 23rd, 1829

Poor Ruby is dead! and before her no more
    From the hearth and the furze-bush the rabbit
        shall rise,—
For her barking is hushed and her bounding is o'er,
    And the birds will hop over the turf where she lies.

And the fire will shine down on the hearthrug at night,
    But poor Ruby will never repose there again,—
For her last sleep has closed up her eyelids, and light
    Will beam bright on her tomb to arouse her in vain.

To the churchyard no more when the service is done
    She will hasten to welcome her master and
        friends,—
Nor again chase her tail round and round in her fun,—
    For with life—Ruby's joy and her liberty ends.—

Poor dog! though the hand which so fondly she loved
    Was the same which in death made her dark eye
        grow dim,—
Yet, had language been hers—she would e'en have
        approved
    Of a deed e'er so fatal—if coming from him!

They'll miss thee—poor Animal! gentle and true,
   In the field and the parlour, [in both thou didst
      shine!]
For 'mongst dogs thou wast good . . . and of mortals,
   how few,
   Can boast of a life half so faultless as thine!—

Thou wilt never come back!—Yet in some future day
   When the grass and the daisies have grown o'er thy
      head—
They will think of thee often at evening—and say
   When they look at thy hearthrug—"Poor Ruby is
      dead!"—

EDWARD LEAR

ON THE DEATH OF A FAVOURITE OLD SPANIEL

Ah, poor companion! when thou followedst last
Thy master's parting footsteps to the gate
Which closed for ever on him, thou didst lose
Thy truest friend, and none was left to plead
For the old age of brute fidelity.
But fare thee well! Mine is no narrow creed;
And He who gave thee being did not frame
The mystery of life to be the sport
Of merciless man! There is another world
For all that live and move—a better one!
Where the proud bipeds, who would fain confine
Infinite Goodness to the little bounds
Of their own charity, may envy thee!

THE PARDON

My dog lay dead five days without a grave
In the thick of summer, hid in a clump of pine
And a jungle of grass and honeysuckle-vine.
I who had loved him while he kept alive

Went only close enough to where he was
To sniff the heavy honeysuckle-smell
Twined with another odor heavier still
And hear the flies' intolerable buzz.

Well, I was ten and very much afraid.
In my kind world the dead were out of range
And I could not forgive the sad or strange
In beast or man. My father took the spade

And buried him. Last night I saw the grass
Slowly divide (it was the same scene
But now it glowed a fierce and mortal green)
And saw the dog emerging. I confess

I felt afraid again, but still he came
In the carnal sun, clothed in a hymn of flies,
And death was breeding in his lively eyes.
I started in to cry and call his name,

Asking forgiveness of his tongueless head.
... I dreamt the past was never past redeeming:
But whether this was false or honest dreaming
I beg death's pardon now. And mourn the dead.

ALI

Small dog named for a wing
never old and never young

abandoned with your brothers on a beach
when you were scarcely weaned

taken home starving
by one woman with
too many to feed as it was

handed over to another
who tied you out back in the weeds
with a clothesline and fed you if she remembered

on the morning before the eclipse of the moon
I first heard about you over the telephone

only the swellings of insect bites
by then held the skin away from your bones

thin hair matted filthy the color of mud
naked belly crusted with sores
head low frightened silent watching

I carried you home and gave you milk and food
bathed you and dried you

dressed your sores and sat with you
in the sun with your wet head on my leg

we had one brother of yours already
and had named him for the great tree of the islands

we named you for the white shadows
behind your thin shoulders

and for the remainder of the desert
in your black muzzle lean as an Afghan's
and for the lightness of your ways
not the famished insubstance of your limbs

but even in your sickness and weakness
when you were hobbled with pain and exhaustion

an aerial grace a fine buoyancy
a lifting as in the moment before flight

I keep finding why that is your name

the plump vet was not impressed with you
and guessed wrong for a long time
about what was the matter

so that you could hardly eat
and never grew like your brother

small dog wise in your days

never servile never disobedient
and never far

standing with one foot on the bottom stair
hoping it was bedtime

standing in the doorway looking up
tail swinging slowly below sharp hip bones

toward the end you were with us whatever we did

the gasping breath through the night
ended an hour and a half before daylight

the gray tongue hung from your mouth
we went on calling you holding you

feeling the sudden height

W. S. MERWIN   233

LAMENT FOR TOBY,
A FRENCH POODLE

The great Toby is dead,
Courteous and discreet,
He of the noble head,
Remote and tragic air,
He of the trim black feet—
He's gone. He is nowhere.

Yet famous in New Hampshire
As one who fought and killed—
Dog-bane and dog-despair—
That prey that all resign,
The terrible and quilled,
Heraldic porcupine.

He will become a legend,
Black coat and royal nature,
So wounded he was blind,
As on a painted shield
Some lost heroic creature
Who fought and would not yield.

If we were brave as he,
Who'd ask to be wise?
We shall remember Toby:

When human courage fails,
Be dogged in just cause
As he before the quills.

MY BOYHOOD DOG

Boxer, my Boxer,
where do you lie?
Somewhere under
a Poona sky.
Ah! my canine,
total joy
you were to me
when as a boy
we coursed the wind
and ran the while,
no end in sight,
mile after mile.
I was to you
and you to me
locked in a bond
eternally.
They never told me
when you died
to spare me pain
in case I cried.
So then to
those adult fears
denied you then,
my childhood tears.

TO THE DOG BELVOIR

Whom I saw in a Dream Push Baby N.
from under a Brewer's Dray and Die in His Place

The stricken Belvoir raised a paw and said:
I die a perfect gentle quadruped.

ACKNOWLEDGMENTS

Thanks are due to the following copyright holders for their permission to reprint:

W. H. AUDEN: "Talking to Dogs" copyright © 1976 by Edward Mendelson, William Meredith and Monroe K. Spears, Executors of the Estate of W. H. Auden, from *Collected Poems* by W. H. Auden. Used by permission of Random House, Inc. Reprinted in the UK from *Collected Poems* by W. H. Auden by permission of Faber and Faber Ltd. CHARLIE BAXTER: "Dog Kibble" by Charlie Baxter is from *Unleashed: Poems by Writers' Dogs*, edited by Amy Hempel and Jim Shepard, Crown Publishers Inc., New York, 1995. Reprinted with the permission of Darhansoff, Verrill, Feldman. ROBIN BECKER: "Dog-God" and "In Praise of the Basset Hound" are from *The Horse Fair* by Robin Becker, © 2000. Reprinted by permission of the University of Pittsburgh Press. ELIZABETH BISHOP: "Pink Dog" from *The Complete Poems 1927–1979* by Elizabeth Bishop. Copyright © 1979, 1983 by Alice Helen Methfessel. Reprinted by permission of Farrar, Straus and Giroux, LLC. SOPHIE CABOT BLACK: "As She Goes". Used by permission of the author. JILL CIMENT: "Mommy" by Jill Ciment is from *Unleashed: Poems by Writers' Dogs*, edited by Amy

241

INDEX OF AUTHORS

251

Helbing.